THE ART OF TIME

JEAN-LOUIS SERVAN-SCHREIBER

Translated by Franklin Philip

ADDISON-WESLEY PUBLISHING COMPANY, INC.

Reading, Massachusetts · Menlo Park, California · New York
Don Mills, Ontario · Wokingham, England · Amsterdam · Bonn
Sydney · Singapore · Tokyo · Madrid · San Juan

Other Books by Jean-Louis Servan-Schreiber

THE RETURN OF COURAGE
LE POUVOIR D'INFORMER
L'ENTERPRISE À VISAGE HUMAIN
A MI-VIE
QUESTIONNAIRE POUR DEMAIN

Library of Congress Cataloging-in-Publication Data

Servan-Schreiber, Jean-Louis, 1937–
  The art of time.

  Translation of: L'art du temps.
  1. Time management.   I. Title.
TX147.S47133   1988   640′.43   88–14499
ISBN 0–201–07978–x

Cover illustration by Michael McLaughlin
Cover design by Copenhaver Cumpston
Text design by Patricia Dunbar
Set in 11-point Baskerville by Neil W. Kelley

CDEDFGHIJ-DO-89
Third printing, October 1989

CONTENTS

TO THE READER

---◆---

Like all important things in life,
making good use of one's time
is not taught in school

Nor are, to be sure, thinking, loving, self-knowledge and growth, child-rearing, foreign languages (I am referring to results, not intentions), and dying.

Thus, we are all self-taught when it comes to making good use of our time. Society (in the person of an uncle or an aunt) is content to give us a watch on some birthday, along with the usual admonition: "Don't forget to use it, and that way you won't be late for dinner again."

Not long after that, our little in-basket (which, after all, holds only twenty-four hours) begins to fill up—with commuting, meetings, work, appointments, sleeping, telephone calls, meals, books, sports, shopping, sex, reading the papers, feeding the kids, and writing notes, (then, suddenly, "Dammit, Christmas is practically here and I haven't bought a single present!")

Some of us give in to the chaos (although the basket keeps filling up), while others get organized. Most people waver between these two attitudes, and it is for them that I have tried to clarify the nature of time, which is so rarely questioned.

If the following pages contain philosophy, psychology, or principles of organization, this may just be a coincidence, for I do not claim expertise in any of these subjects.

Out of sympathy with the reader, I have also kept this book short, so as not to take up too much of his or her time.

Today, most of us have a problem managing our time and are unaware that the problem is treatable.

Opinion polls conducted in the industrialized countries show that people complain more about a lack of time than a lack of money, greenery, or freedom. Could this be the evil of our era?

Time is life much more than it is money. We cannot resign ourselves to an ailment that undermines our effectiveness and our serenity.

Dear homo sapiens—dear reader —you are marvelous and indefatigable. In the past one hundred fifty years you have gained control over your health, physical well-being, speed, communications, space, and now your body.

Your next challenge is obvious—the conquest of your time.

It will not be easy, for in this area science and technology are of little help, and so the struggle will be barehanded. The effort is worth the trouble, however, for it may lead to the even more wonderful conquest of wisdom.

MODERN TIME

◆

It was in Singapore a few years ago that modern time first came to my attention. It was there I purchased the latest in Japanese digital watches from one of those emporia offering six floors of electronic equipment and pearls. As the watch blinked off each second suddenly it seemed that it was my own time that was being inexorably measured.

Up to then, I had worn unthreatening types of watches, with sweep-second hands like those on the clocks and pocket watches of centuries past on which time goes round like a tethered horse circling its trainer. In this circularity of minutes and hours, duration rolls around itself like the planet and the galaxy. Unalterably.

The first watches to display numerals, luminous or not, were no more worrisome. Like airport clocks, they announced the hours and minutes without shifting. You detected only the sudden change of the last four numerals; time appeared to change even less than on the round dial.

With the uncannily precise quartz watches, however, it seemed absurd not to know the time to the half minute, and the Japanese electronic engineers soon remedied that lack. The not very attractive metallic object I had just bought from a Chinese clerk had six numerals: two for the hour, two for the minute, two for the second. From then on, before my very eyes, the seconds slipped away at full speed.

I learned that the writer Jean-Louis Bory, who also wore this latest device, said to a friend, shortly before committing suicide: "This watch you see is my death." I had the same feeling going back to my Singapore hotel. On my wrist, time no longer turned around, it frittered away. Each second sent the preceding one into the void, and me along with it. The illusion of circular time came to an end; unrelentingly, linear time clutched me by the arm.

Westerners are so made (by education, not birth) that, when faced with a problem, they like to ask some preliminary questions. Because we feel a need "to gain better mastery of our time," our logical programming first impels us to play with some key notions.

Mastery is both relative and subjective, but we will discuss that further on. Do we know exactly what time is?

> Of course we do. It's what goes by between the day a friend is supposed to repay a loan and the day you actually get the money.

> Certainly, but we prefer more general definitions. So, what is time?

> Just a minute! There's a prior question. Are you sure time exists?

Now there's a dumb question. Obviously, you only have to see how worn the living-room carpet has become!

Not just that. It shows us a limit; if nothing ever changed, if everything in the world and in us remained immobile and constant, wouldn't we say that time had been abolished?

Maybe, but that's not the way things are. And I'm a little hungry.

Some people think otherwise. The Hindus who believe in reincarnation and the Eternal Return believe that everything always begins again and so time is just an illusion.

Buddhists too, I gather. But, being a practical people, they add that since we live in a world where this illusion predominates, it is important for each thing to be done at its proper time.

To choose the simplest definition of time, couldn't we say that it is what measures a transformation?

The transformation of a raw egg to a soft-boiled one takes four minutes; the transformation of carbon 14 is measured in thousands of years. Between these are you and I inclined to judge time according to the rhythm of our own transformation: short run, long run? "In the long run," noted the economist John Maynard Keynes, "we are all dead."

We see our time against the background of our death. Nature provided our primitive ancestors with few other signs of the passage of time. They saw realities in which change was scarcely detectable (lakes, mountains) or that seemed to reproduce identical versions of themselves (day and nights, the return of the seasons, animals).

Some millennia before the invention of water clocks and hour glasses, the first instrument for measuring time may well have been rheumatoid arthritis, the irritating reminder of our internal modification.

The next instrument was no doubt the mirror (still waters or polished metal), silent witness to our deterioration. The passage of time is and always will be a personal experience or drama; the hardest thing about aging is that one remains inwardly youthful. "Every tragedy we can imagine," philosophized Simone Weil, "comes back to just one: time slipping by."

We have no great liking for the idea of transformation. If we have so long inscribed time on dials, we perhaps want to go on believing in the circular time of our ancestors.

A stabbing pain in the kidneys, an early morning glance in the mirror, seconds escaping from a quartz watch: the signs of time's flight give us little pleasure but at least lead us to reflect.

Our popular ways of expressing ourselves can be misleading. "Gaining" or "losing" time makes no sense: we have the totality of available time at our disposal. It is unmodifiable. The only thing we can do about it is change our attitude toward it and make good or poor use of it. And that is indeed something.

The following major truth flows from that fact: to get time under control involves getting oneself under control. Worse luck for those hoping for tricks or miracles.

Although we can raise philosophical doubts about time or consider it merely the evidence of entropy, its practical role is that of an essential resource— one with special characteristics.

Like any resource, time is available and designed to be used. It is the most democratically distributed resource: every person has exactly the same amount of time available, no matter whether he or she is powerful or poor, enterprising or idle, bright or stupid. It is clearly our most precious resource, for it is the only nonrenewable one.

The paradox of time is that people rarely consider they have enough when in fact all of it is available to everyone.

Unlike other resources, time cannot be bought or sold, borrowed or stolen, stocked up or saved, manufactured, reproduced, or modified. All we can do is make use of it. And whether we use it or not, it nevertheless slips away.

But these are mere conceptual considerations. What we need are some practical and operational ideas about time. The well-known relation between space and time may prove helpful here, for we grasp spatial demonstrations more easily than temporal ones.

Whether or not time is a fourth dimension, we realize that it is related to such a referential system. For certain distances to be meaningful, we prefer to express them in time (as in several days' walk, hours by plane, or light-years) rather than in miles. Perhaps it would be useful to do the reverse and relate our time to some space.

Imagine that each of us lived in a room of exactly the same size, with no possibility of enlarging the present one. Thus, the only thing differentiating us would be the way in which we filled up the room.

Some people—insecure or ostentatious—would buy a great deal of furniture and eventually notice that they could barely get about in the congestion.

Others, although accumulating less stuff, would arrange theirs in such disorder that they would feel disoriented and cramped.

Others, however, fitting out wardrobes, sets of drawers, and bookshelves, would manage to get this space to hold the things they needed while still leaving room for moving about freely.

For space, then, we see that under the same conditions each person's tendencies and temperament decides his or her style of living. It is the same with time.

But before considering the unique and personal manner in which we each inhabit time, let us look at the type of time we encounter in the here and now—a developed country toward the end of the twentieth century.

The present time—modern time—is unified, rhythmic, and congested.

Unified, for the whole planet is synchronized to the nearest thousandth of a second; only the numbers assigned to the hours change, depending on the time zone. The time signal is now identical all over the globe as it is in space.

Rhythmic, for we are bound by a network of social habits whose links are reckoned in time. We follow schedules for work, meetings, meals, hours of business, the TV morning news or evening movie, plane flights, and infants' feedings.

Congested, for physical existence in this complex

society has forced us to become busier and more productive than our forebears. This huge increase in output means we must perform more activities in the fixed amount of time allotted to us.

All this is quite recent. If we had been living a hundred fifty years ago, we most likely would have been peasants leading a life not unlike that of peasants centuries before. Certainly, as distinct from their predecessors, they could know what time it was. They had no watches (too intricate and expensive), but the church bell sounded for morning, noon, and evening prayers.

The time was then very approximate, for each town, even each village, practiced its own. Each province thus covered thousands of different times. Sometimes, when politics got mixed in, the church bell signaled a different hour from the clock on the town hall.

In that life, time was closer in nature to that of a cat: its rhythm set by the sun and consisting of periods of uninterrupted activities. We often think of those times nostalgically even though we feel they must have been, by our fidgety standards, singularly boring.

The first strain came with the first appointment: reporting for outside work. When factories and mines transformed the sons and daughters of peasants into workers, they had to leave their homes each morning to reach the boss's door by some specified time, on pain of losing the job.

This was the first and basic diversion in the flow of natural time. More than the light of the sun, entering and leaving the factory set the daily rhythm. Between these two moments it was forbidden to know the time and thus to carry a watch. The boss was the lone master of the effective duration of the day imposed on his employees.

In a few decades, the cutting up of life into a schedule accelerated as more had to be produced.

In the workplace the clock gave way to the chronometer. Because the workers no longer produced their own food or clothing, they had to adapt to the hours of the people selling these things to them. When, finally and much later, they could introduce some leisure into their lives, they also needed to be on time for the start of a show or concert.

That is how, without realizing it, civilized people came to find themselves like Gulliver among the Lilliputians, tied down by a multitude of subtle bonds, none of which is individually strong enough to immobilize them, but which together deprive them of their freedom of movement.

During the same period—the second half of the nineteenth century—the railroad and later the radio, brought about the universal synchronization of time.

Alone on his island Robinson Crusoe had no need for a watch. But as soon as a community is formed, its common activities (meals, meetings, religious services) have to be regulated. Before industrialization, however, an approximate sequence of activities in each village still sufficed.

As the railroads established regional, national, and soon international networks, people had to predict the arrival and departure times of trains over thousands of miles and thus needed to create a single time system. For some years, the train-station clock did not necessarily tally with the one on the church steeple. It was already foreseeable, however, that the station clock would eventually win out.

Soon, the development of radio communication required not only synchronization, but also precision. Universal time is precise to the millionth of a second, thanks to the quartz. The watch is the most-produced object in the world: four hundred million a year. The obsession with the right time has become a mass preoccupation: in Paris, the number of telephone calls for the time runs to nearly 400,000 a day! Hence the French philosopher, Michel Serres's statement: "From now on everyone has a watch and no one has the time. Exchange one for the other: give away your watch and take your time."

It's too late for that. Or rather too soon, for Serres is talking about the ultimate luxury for a society of abundance.

There already are laboratories on every continent for testing this solution: the villages of the Club Med. They meet the three conditions necessary:

1. A small community needing no relations to the outside,

2. Where everything is provided in abundance,

3. And the individual is not forced to do anything, not even to get out of bed.

But to afford this experience for a week or two every year, watch wearers are all the more obliged, the rest of the time, to personal productivity based on precise timing.

A new paradox about time: our present standard of living is incomparably higher and more comfortable than that of our peasant forebears. In comparison with the labors of the early industrial worker, our own workdays are half as long and our days off have doubled. Yet we feel much more rushed than they.

Here we reach the heart of the problem. Something unexpected happened along the way, predicted by nineteenth-century utopians from Charles Fourier to Karl Marx. Confident in the blessings of progress, they proclaimed an abundance that would liberate human beings from the awful servitude of the early mills and factories and the enslavement of child labor.

In the industrialized countries abundance has become the rule together with a spectacular reduction in working hours. (In France, with five weeks of annual vacation and a thirty-nine-hour work week, work represents no more than 1,883 of the 8,730 hours in a year, or one in five.) This reduction was accompanied by an invasion of timesaving devices: the automobile, household appliances, the telephone, prepared foods. Yet the result is the opposite of what the visionaries imagined. We have more time available, and yet we feel we have less of it.

And that's the main problem nowadays. In 1981 French workers were polled on their chief "sources of frustration." At the head of the list, with 43 percent, was time. Money, second on the list, came far behind, with 27 percent.

Nevertheless, we should not fall into the old trap of blaming this on "society." The mastery of time is our business and we alone are responsible for it. To confront it squarely, however, we need to understand what about the structure of modern time affects nearly all of us.

We ought also to keep in mind that our era has won some victories over immutable time that, although partial, enable us to make more intelligent use of it. These come down to practical details, clever arrangements of the identical room in which each of us lives.

One example is the Concorde, a financial disaster, but a fabulous symbol of modern time. It is the first commercial product with which man realizes a dream as old as that of flying: going back in time.

After taking off from Charles de Gaulle Airport in Paris at 11:00 A.M., the Concorde lands at Kennedy at 8:00 A.M., enabling some one hundred privileged persons to arrive three hours before they left. The fact that these 180 minutes "gained" have cost each traveler the equivalent of three months of the French minimum monthly wage does not prevent them from feeling they have gained a symbolic triumph over time.

Symbolic only, for they have not turned back the hands of the true clock, their biological one. But for want of having been rejuvenated by three hours, they have treated themselves to the most luxurious means of mastering time.

To maximize the Concorde effect, some executives leave their Paris office after an hour's work on Monday morning. They land in New York at the start of the American work day, which they make full use of before heading back to Paris on the regular 7:00 P.M. flight, where they buy three tourist-class seats (for the same price as one on the supersonic flight); then they stretch out and sleep for six hours. On Tuesday morning, they are back to work in their Paris office, free from fatigue and jet lag.

Working Monday on Park Avenue and Tuesday on the Champs-Elysées, they have overcome not time, but distance, through optimal use of their time.

A clever arrangement of closets, trunks, and shelves allows a mariner to stow a month's provisions and all his gear in the tiny cabin of his sailboat. In the same way, most modern inventions aim at enabling us to accomplish more in a fixed amount of time.

The latest technological goal: doing the same thing in less time. A car gets you to work in a tenth the time it would take a horse. A microwave oven cooks a chicken ten times faster than a conventional oven. All the machines and systems that took a week to produce a certain number of cars thirty years ago now take a week. And there are a thousand other innovations still to come.

Another approach is to do several things at once. This is generally achieved by combining some physical activity with a mental one although mixing two intellectual tasks can lead to confusion or inattention. The radio allows us to get information while we are shaving; trains and planes take us somewhere while we are reading or sleeping. The most basic manipulation of time is the transformation—first by means of codes, then with machines—of the time lag in communication between two individuals.

For you to listen to a symphony conceived in Mozart's mind two centuries ago, the composer first had to use a code, musical notation. Later, say, some ten years ago, an orchestra assembled to decode this notation and to re-create the music. The recording enables you to hear the symphony, benefiting from a double jump in time: from the moment of Mozart's creation and from that of the orchestra's performance.

This is especially true of writing, the most widespread code that has allowed ideas and words to outlive their author. In this regard a library resembles the heavens that simultaneously strike our retinas with the light emitted by a star a century ago or by a galaxy a million years ago. In the same way, from between the covers of books comes a message from Plato framed some 2,500 years ago, another from Pascal some three hundred years old, and a third from William Faulkner written merely thirty years ago.

It is writing and not printing that enables people to separate the genesis of an idea from its perception. Gutenberg introduced not an effect in time, but in space.

More recently, new machines have greatly magnified our power to introduce delays between production and enjoyment—the freezer, which allows us to consume a dish cooked a week earlier; the VCR, which allows us to watch on Thursday a movie televised the previous Sunday. There, we do not change the duration, but we can manipulate the order and moment.

A great deal of technical progress has almost completely eliminated the time required by certain acts: the telephone that spares the caller or a courier the time to travel to the destination; the washing machine that substitutes for scrubbing; the computer that functions communicatively like a telephone and also substitutes for mental labor, calculating, drawing, supervising, or placing orders in our stead.

Special mention should be made of money, whose

close connection with time is most often expressed as "time is money." Now, the reverse is equally true. Money in a savings account represents the depositor's working time, and his or her enjoyment of what it can provide may be postponed (he or she may save for a vacation, for retirement, or the like).

Obviously, however, the connection that develops between money and the time available to us is ambiguous. On the one hand, this connection gives our desires a way of coming true and so draws on our capital time; on the other hand, the connection makes time management easier, for we can purchase timesaving machines that immediately become indispensable.

When we recognize this ambiguity we realize that money is just a neutral tool to be used well or poorly. It is time that remains the central problem, for in the last analysis time is what measures our life.

Philosophically, this has been true in every time and place. For all people, the use of time has ever been closely connected with the meaning of life. Save for philosophers, however, few people have been truly aware of this—until time became a scarce resource.

Preoccupation with time has become universal, which indicates genuine progress. We are henceforth obliged to consider and to study the very fabric of our existence.

To see how modern time is profoundly different from that experienced by our ancestors is to understand that progress has treated time in much the same way it has treated nature—it has used both unreflectively as if there were a limitless supply.

Water, air, greenery, beauty, and time were greedily

exploited for a hundred fifty years before it was realized how irreplaceable and vital they are.

It is up to each of us to experience the revolution in favor of nature promoted by ecologists (the battle is far from being won) in connection with our own personal use of time.

CONGESTED TIME

◆

*Television's 10 percent • The race to produce
Consumption takes time • The charter flight, rather than
the culture • Relearning pleasure • A longer life with
multiple times • Encounter with the times of others
The king of time-savers • Seven minutes for reflection
The phobia of waiting • Love in two minutes
A dietetics of time*

In the early 1950s television in Europe and America was a rare phenomenon. Today, everyone has a set and watches it an average of two and a half hours a day, some 10 percent of the inextensible number of hours in a day.

Now, the past four decades have not seen a shortening of the work week. So on top of our forty work hours, television's 10 percent of the week's hours are taken from the hours remaining—either *instead of* activities like sleep, recreation, reading, and puttering, or *along with* meals, family time, work around the house, but always *at the expense of* things like conversation, affectivity, concentration, and inner calm.

Now, although we need to work in order to eat, and to sleep in order to rest, none of us "needs" to watch television. So if we explain this to someone who watches television several evenings a week and yet complains (it's common) of a lack of time for reading or getting enough sleep, will he or she immediately give up television? The bets are open.

The technology that offers us instruments for freeing up our time (we don't have to travel to a theater to enjoy a movie) has also perfected ones that gobble up the extra time thus created.

The present congestion of time results first from the increased level of our demands. But it also has economic causes: productivity, scattering, and consumption.

Productivity demands that we accomplish an ever-increasing number of tasks in a necessarily fixed amount of time to ensure economic growth and maintain the complexities of developed societies.

Certainly, machines have continually reduced our workload, filling in for physical effort and encouraging much quicker and more frequent communications. But the lessons of the years since the Second World War show that our demand for products, services, or financial rewards always rises faster than the increase in the output of machines—during periods of rapid economic growth or, as in the early 1980s, periods of slower economic expansion.

Even during slowdowns in economic growth, the need for increased productivity stays the same in order to maintain a certain profit margin despite the slump in sales. This then creates the unemployed, who find they have free time they could well do without. But people who still have work find themselves with just that much more to do, and they live under greater tension.

Scattering or dispersion adds to the strain of professional life and is chiefly expressed in commuting time. Not only is the workplace dissociated from where we live, but the distance between home and job is increasing. In addition, the modern supermarkets are not likely to be found around the block, our children don't necessarily walk to a neighborhood school, our parents live halfway across the continent, our doctor has his or her office across town, and we often travel miles to a movie theater complex, downtown theater district, or the beach.

Many unfortunate suburbanites face three to four hours of daily commuting. Every day most of us—urbanite and suburbanite—spend a large part of the hours freed up by modern timesaving appliances and the shorter work week in unproductive traveling.

Certainly, the telephone, mail-order catalogues, and personal computers spare us a good deal of running around, but urbanization and specialization of neighborhoods makes shopping, entertainment, and business and personal errands more time consuming.

Finally, the latest and least-expected constriction of our time is in *consumption*. Economists failed to take account of one fact: it takes time to consume. The increase in our purchasing power allowed each of us to step up his or her consumption, but the time available for this consumption has not increased correspondingly.

Faced with a major purchase, everyone thinks of determining the price, the method of financing, and perhaps the quality. But who considers the budget of time inevitably connected to it: choosing, enjoying, repairing, and maintaining it?

Choice: the profusion and increasing technical complexity of the objects offered us should lead the rational consumer (whom we claim to be) to precede every purchase with a comparative study of prices and performances. Did you do this before you chose your car, your VCR, or your dishwasher?

For lack of time, the more lavish and complicated the choice of products, the poorer the quality of our buying decision. With our tacit consent, advertising influences our decisions. We ignorant consumers rely on clever ads to relieve our guilt by murmuring arguments that we then adopt at the moment of purchase.

Maintenance: how much time does a boat owner spend sandpapering it or rigging it up compared with the time he is out sailing it? How much time does a pool owner spend swimming and cleaning it? How much time do you need to keep up your country house compared with the actual leisure time you spend there?

If the cost of our second homes was divided by the number of days we actually spend in them (not forgetting the interest on the money tied up in frozen assets), we might realize that for the same length of time we could rent the most sumptuous villas on the Riviera and still have money to put aside.

And for those people who feel they do take advantage of their second home, do they ever feel a yearning for trips that the time spent in their house "to make worthwhile use of it" stops them from taking?

Enjoyment: rise up, books never read, records listened to just once, suits scarcely worn, VCR cassettes recorded but never played back! Our attics are full of roller skates, rowing machines, and bicycles bought on an impulse with no thought of the number of hours it would take to actually use them.

From the viewpoint of time utilization, consumption is our century's great neurosis, at least if we use the least clinical definition of neurosis as "someone intelligent doing something stupid."

The intelligence of Henry Ford (who started out as a watchmaker) lay in his paying his workers enough wages for them to afford one of the cars they produced. Our stupidity is that of adopting Ford's principle at our own expense. We rush to spend our earnings on the objects and services we produce, and only afterward do we think about living better.

We think much more about the use of our money, which is renewable, than we do about the use of our time, which is irreplaceable.

Thus, our bulimia of consumption not only eats into our time, but it eats itself. Our skills at consuming remain primitive.

We switch on our ever more sophisticated sound systems to create a background noise to which we then listen with only half our attention. We end up finding music gratifying only as an accompaniment to some other activity. There is no time for creating at home the conditions to really absorb and savor the music.

We eat quickly and in great quantity heavy products cooked in haste. There is no time for doing one's grocery shopping with care, cooking with love, relishing fine foods.

To set off for the ends of the earth we concentrate on tracking down the cheapest charter flight, rather than reading up about the culture and problems of the countries we're about to visit. Once there, we look at faces and landscapes—through the lens of our Nikon rather than live. And once we're back, no time to look at the photos whose taking prevented us from appreciating the journey.

We get together with our friends at dinner parties or noisy, crowded receptions where, because of this, conversation is leveled to the least common denominator. No time to see them one by one, two by two, to truly know who they are, how they live and think.

It generally meets with approval to criticize the "consumer society." But is this for ethical reasons or because the consumer society has not brought us the anticipated satisfactions? In fact, the chief cause of this lack of satisfaction has to do with poor use of the time for consumptions that leads us to telescope them or to pile them up.

People in the developed countries behave like the nouveaux riches, eager to take advantage of what they can finally acquire.

We devote bits of time to a multitude of pleasures instead of enjoying at leisure the rare ones that genuinely suit us.

Shouldn't we first determine our needs and desires?

What are the facts and figures? It takes some 40 percent of the hours in a day to satisfy our vital, biological needs: sleeping (seven hours), eating (two hours), dressing and personal care and hygiene (one hour)—ten hours in all. To be able to provide this (as well as housing, heating, and medical need), we must have money and so must work (eight hours plus one hour getting to and from the job)—nine hours. So, today the time devoted to needs is on the order of nineteen hours a day (twenty to twenty-one if we add a minimum of shopping and housework). Thus, we have three to four hours to spare for our desires (family life, entertainment, learning, sports, and so on). If we sacrifice two and a half hours to "television's 10 percent," the remaining time reduces to some thirty to ninety minutes.

Not a lot, is it? But we should recall our past patterns. At the start of the industrial era, workers worked twelve hours and, to recuperate, slept at least one hour more than we. Their time for needs thus took up the whole twenty-four hour day. Nothing left for the pleasures of life. Which was just as well, since they hadn't a cent for satisfying them.

In relation to our forebears, we have real free time, while the income from our work lets us afford to satisfy much more than just our biological needs.

The trouble is that although we can just about satisfy our more expensive needs (you don't eat three steaks a day), can we say the same about satisfying our desires, which everything today tends to stimulate: education, advertising, the permanent display of more attractive styles of life?

The reflex of mimicry on which the Stanford-based philosopher René Girard bases our behavior has stimulated a giant industry, that of envy. We have become more refined, more imaginative, more prosperous— how is it we are not more demanding? On the one hand, thus a revolution of desires; on the other, just a few hours in which to satisfy them. Let's not look elsewhere for the basic reasons for a sense of having too little time:

our desires have increased much more quickly than the available time.

But the congestion of time is not the result of a mere subjective impression. It is true, in addition, that the present era has pitilessly hacked it up into small pieces. Our slices of time get narrower and narrower, and this segmentation has a determining influence on our behavior.

Until very recently, the individual lived in well-defined pigeonholes: one spouse, one employer, one home—often for life. In these three domains, the very idea of change and mobility met with general disapproval. Life went on in these well-defined molds, without surprise.

Following the end of the Second World War, everything very quickly changed.

Still, for most of us, multiple moves cut our lifetimes into geographical slices, changes of employer into professional slices, successive partners into emotional slices. And the not necessarily simultaneous combination of the three provides many excuses for those who sometimes get muddled in their memories.

For a short life with few times we substituted a long life with multiple and mixed times.

But what most fractionates our time (to the point of atomizing it) are the constant interferences with the time of other people—because there are more of them, because they have easier access to us, because the pressure on us to respond to them gets stronger and stronger.

Cast a pebble into a calm pond. Perfect concentric circles lazily expand out until calm returns to the surface. But let a hailstorm rage, peppering the surface, and thousands of circles intersect and form a chaotic infinitude of wavelets. The water becomes turbid. That is how the time of others scrambles up our own.

Rural time, in our not so distant past, was the calm pond: few encounters, few interactions. Towns stayed small, like the work units that they harbored.

Today, even if it happens that we feel alone in a crowd, the crowd hems us in. In the megalopolises we live in, the businesses we work in, we come into daily contact with hundreds of our peers.

It is estimated that we each know an average of some one thousand people. Even though only a hundred of them has regular effective access to us (family, coworkers, friends, service people, clients, neighbors, relatives, and so forth), these are just so many occasions for interruptions, for fractionated and successive concentrations. Without realizing it, each person who enters into communication with us is preying on our precious and irreplaceable time. As we are of his or hers.

There is an ambiguity here. Few of us are cut out for living in solitude, and to mix our time with that of others is precisely what we are seeking.

But as in nearly every area, the abuse of a pleasure makes it first into an annoyance and then into a nightmare. Having friends into dinner one night a week is delightful. Three nights a week is exhausting. Every night would be hell.

So is our common experience that beyond a certain number of children, coworkers, and friends the problem of time doesn't even arise, since it is wholly consumed by them?

There again, modern life has speeded up the phenomenon. Not only has it put us in contact with many more of our peers, but it has given them the means of cornering us more easily.

In the era of the handwritten letter delivered on foot or on horseback, how many messages were sent and received each day? How many visits by horse and carriage or voyages by boat could one accomplish?

The crack ocean liner *Normandie* took six days each way crossing the North Atlantic. What friendships or idylls must have occurred on board! What books read, pages written, poker games won or lost! No way, once at sea, to be telephoned. A forced truce in the stress.

Today we fly to New York for the afternoon, to London for the weekend. Because of the speed of modern transport, we are creating in several places on the earth networks of connection that will have in their turn access to us.

Among the perverse effects of progress, we can establish that everything that facilitates communication further atomizes our time. If Aesop were alive, he would say that the best and the worst of things is not the language, but its omnipresent and unscrupulous appendage: the telephone.

Thanks to the telephone, anyone may barge right into the midst of your crucial negotiation, family dinner, creative thought, sleep, shower, moments of tenderness.

In the earliest days of the telephone, just a hundred years ago, sensible people kept their capacity to take offense. The French actor Lucien Guitry, born in 1860, said disdainfully: "Someone rings you like a servant and you answer?"

On the contrary, today the king of time-savers is the object of universal admiration. In the past few years, a diabolical technology has even allowed it to reach its target—ourselves—with the inexorability of a Minute-man missile.

Answering machines make certain that no call will fail to get through to us. "Call-through" devices allow pests to hound us at our friends' or in another office. "Call-waiting" mechanisms produce delightful interruptions by another call when we are in midconversation. Light, portable receivers track us in the last refuges for reflection: car, lawn, bathroom.

Soon, finally, thanks to cellular radios, the telephone will be kept in one's pocket. Wherever we are on the planet, we will be plugged in, connected, and well and truly strung up to others.

Our days become sieves, due to the combination of three factors: the economic necessity of assuming more numerous and diverse tasks; the considerable increase in the number of people with whom we enter into contact; the availability of the means of communication and of plentiful, cheap transportation to these people. All these are more than sufficient to transform the flesh of our time into chopped meat.

Alas, it is not merely a metaphor. Studies of the work day of managers at every level have shown that their average uninterrupted stretch of time doesn't last over seven or eight minutes. The "one minute" manager is for real. It is pointless under these conditions to claim you are still reflecting.

We may be distressed that our civilization has led *homo* so-called *sapiens* to this absurdity. We may even admire our adaptability to this neurosis. But the interesting question is: Why do we do so little about it?

"Man can stand anything," suggested the nineteenth-century French poet Count Lautréamont, "provided it lasts but a second." What if, on the pretext that we are too busy, it suited us to have no time to think?

What if we created this swarming society because it corresponded to a profound human tendency: a diversion that keeps us from noticing the passing of time?

Time torments us. We luxuriate in it so as to forget it, then we speed up to leave it behind. And what does it matter, after all, for the interval between a declaration of nuclear war and the end of the world would be about a quarter of an hour?

Even if this madness is unconsciously willed, it in turn produces troubling changes in the modern individual: like the inability to wait or to concentrate.

As early as 1907, the French philosopher Henri Bergson noted: "If I want a glass of sugar water I have got to wait for the sugar to melt." He would surely be relieved to note that, thanks to modern technology, our sugar cube dissolves nowadays much more quickly. But it still takes more than a second.

The futurologist Herman Kahn recalled that when as a child he asked for a bicycle, he got the following answer: "A bicycle's expensive. Maybe next year." He noted that for his own grandson "next year" would be tantamount to saying "never."

The most sophisticated communication has become the television commercial, for everything must be said in thirty seconds. On a computer, a response time of five seconds is experienced as interminable. We trade in the machine for a more responsive one.

Educational researchers have also measured how long a teacher who has just asked a pupil a question waits before he gets the impression that the pupil is not going to answer. The feeling comes in less than one second.

After a Concorde landing in New York, an on-board electrical failure kept the exit door stuck shut for a time. At the end of seven minutes, the passengers were figuring what they were going to demand by way of indemnities from Air France. After fifteen minutes, they were on the verge of rioting.

This chronic impatience has, moreover, the most pernicious effect on our ability to concentrate. Our idea takes account only of the time to do, to act it; that of reflection—before and after—has vanished into thin air. Most decisions are made on the spot, by intuition, in a flash, like Dr. Balint's diagnoses.

We pay expensive consultants to study problems that we may well understand better than they, but have given up thinking about.

Sprinters of action, we lack the wind for the long-distance race of reflection.

In business as in politics, decision makers no longer work with firsthand data that they themselves have gathered and analyzed. They get used to referring to conclusions and summaries by experts (market studies, commission reports) who often have different values or standards.

The skittish approach of modern time leads to doing nothing thoroughly, just so we can do more of it. How many people prefer to race through two daily papers or weekly new magazines rather than to give one a thorough reading? If we multiplied the number of books sold (sharply on the increase) by the number of hours required to read them, we obtain utterly improbable figures. Moreover, beyond reminiscences, on which subjects do we think we are cultivated?

With prosperity, the connoisseur of art has been replaced by the collector, for someone can acquire a collection at the same time as he is getting rich, but it takes months or even years to absorb a subject.

Our impatience also makes us superficial, as though to avoid asking ourselves simple and thus profound questions. And when despite this, we suddenly wonder about our reasons for acting or living, we call this an existential crisis.

Our obsession with the "how much" and "how" keeps us at a comfortable distance from the "why."

Time-chopping spares nothing, not even love. Is it merely by chance that the "sexual revolution" coincided with the proliferation of fast-food restaurants? Doesn't this revolution compare to the art of loving the same way the hamburger compares to haute cuisine?

Here again, we have to speed up to conform to the pull of time. Courting means using outmoded circumlocutions and patience. Maintaining a relationship requires an investment of time whose productivity is now doubtful.

Now, the true raw material of love is time. "It is unfortunately true," said the poet Charles Baudelaire, "that without leisure love becomes merely a common man's debauch. Instead of burning or dreamy caprice, it becomes a repulsive utility."

Romance has foundered in a calculus of profitability. One cool character in the British film *The Knack* declared he "needed only two minutes from start to finish [to make love]." People who bemoan the fact that women have become "easy" are doing them a grave injustice. They are merely demonstrating their adaptability.

Up to this point we have measured the extent to which modern life abuses the ancestral, natural time by which humanity believed itself firmly defined. Destabilized and giddy and sometimes breathless at the changes around us, we wonder whether we can ever regain our lost equilibrium.

Individually, of course, this reconquest involves a dawning awareness and achievement of mastery, a genuine re-education that is the purpose of this book.

We have the most urgent need for a time "diet" and none is really available.

In the industrialized countries, when perpetual scarcity of food was succeeded by relative abundance, the people did not resist. They began gorging themselves and grew fat. Many died as a result. Then they looked at each other and found their bodies ugly and uncomfortable. So reaction set in in the form of articles, books, programs, and word of mouth until the removal of excess weight became a universal preoccupation.

The matter is well under way, and our bodies already are less flabby than they once were. A much broader proportion of young people have been raised according to a few simple principles they have adopted as their own. Their new approach to a simple, healthier, more nutritious, diet is beginning to influence the whole population.

Unfortunately, the poor use of our time does not make us fat, and so its effects are less visible. That may be why the problem has not yet been given national priority.

Nevertheless, it can make us as sick as overeating. Ulcers, heart attacks, and cancers are created in the furrows of stress, which is to time what obesity is to food.

In a sense, this situation is much more serious, because many more people suffer from stress than from obesity. Because, although one can be fat and still be happy people without enough time rarely experience the joy of living. Let's begin by attempting to understand how, personally, we reached this point.

EXPERIENCED TIME

———————◆———————

Chewing gum time • Hours are becoming scarce
Our children already pressured • Managing to be on time
The fundamental experience of the present
The temporal horizon • Enlarging the future
Freedom and organization • The time things actually take
Why Mitterand is late.

Whether you have two weeks or two months, at a certain point in your vacation, time begins to accelerate. At first, the end seems far off. You can afford not to think about it. You feel you have a wealth of leisure, like someone whose bank account is so full he needn't figure the balance. Bits of eternity.

You can still fantasize about doing it all: reading three books, going on a two-day trip, taking up windsurfing, playing chess with the kids, talking into the night with friends. Dreamed-of time is expandable and accommodates all this with ease.

This sense that time's course has slackened is the chief benefit we expect from a vacation: to break the rhythm, to regain our availability.

Then, inevitably, reality comes back at a gallop. Once again we see we are approaching the horizon: the end of vacation. The remaining days take on different dimensions. They shrink and cannot hold everything we'd planned for them. We are still on vacation, but we must now perform a triage.

We decide which book will remain unopened; we give up on the trip. Although not yet back in harness, our total freedom is gone.

When does this tilt occur? For the fainthearted, after two days; for the happy-go-lucky types, the last evening. For me, it happens around the midpoint, whenever that is.

It is the same, of course, with life. At the age of ten, a year seems a century; at forty, a brief interlude. The subjective duration of time varies in the course of life.

Up to now, we have described a solid, unyielding, and electronic time, and suddenly we realize it can be distorted like chewing gum. Is it still the same time?

No, of course not. To understand the rest of this book, we must realize that we live to a triple beat: nature's time, society's time, and experienced time—our own.

Nature's time is cosmic time, that of the fifteen billion years since the Big Bang. We are still unsure whether the universe will go on expanding indefinitely or contract back into infinite density until some creative new explosion of other worlds. On a more modest scale, natural time is also that of our suburban solar system, with day and night, cold and warmth, green and white.

Whether natural time is one of universal entropy or the Eternal Return remains unsettled. It will excite future generations of physicists and metaphysicians. And while some people may suggest that natural time does not exist, this is of little consequence. For it goes so far beyond us or seems so repetitive that it has little influence on our earthly life. This time doesn't give a damn whether the planet has human beings on it.

Society's time, modern time, on the other hand, holds us in its close embrace. Arising from the proliferation and acceleration of interpersonal relations, it is a convention. Transported to a desert island, one would immediately cast off these oppressive social garments.

Made up of interlocking codes and practices, social time is omnipresent in our existence; it sets the pace of our activity in every sphere. But it enters the individual from the outside and is not that individual. To keep from being alienated or overwhelmed by it, we clearly have a stake in knowing the rules and management of time. For skilled players, the winnings may be substantial, for they add up to freedom.

Experienced time is, of course, intimately mingled with social time, yet we must not confuse the two. Consisting of perceptions, feelings, and biology, experienced time is—for us humans, at any rate—the most real of the three times. Perceived duration is the very stuff of personal lives and not definable by the codes of social time. Coupled terms like *long* or *short*, *quiet* or *crazy*, *exciting* or *dreary* describe it better than *minute*, *week*, or *year*. Social time is quantifiable, while experienced time is expressed through its quality.

In experienced time, an hour or a year does not have the same subjective duration, for it varies in length depending on one's stage of life or one's circumstances. In the final analysis it is, of course, experienced time that is the most real and most vital to us. It is the time of affectivity, creation, the enjoyment of thinking and knowing. It is as fragile as it is essential, for it is interlaced with social time, which, like a clinging vine, may end up choking the host plant.

It is experienced time that to different degrees we feel is lacking; to some it is merely a memory.

We noted earlier that as we grow older time seems to shrink. Here we are clearly dealing with experienced time. It is beyond the age of thirty that this shrinking begins. First through the increasing demands of external pressure: Because of an unfortunate timing, one's weightiest professional responsibilities coincide with the most exacting family obligations. The room quickly fills up, leaving us scarcely any space to maneuver in.

It is often the case that in these years a certain critical inner event occurs: we realize we're going to die. As during our vacation the horizon of the holiday's end suddenly appeared, so we lose the confidence in our immortality that's so natural to the young.

The realization that our stock of time is limited, non-renewable and each day irrevocably amputated suddenly gives to each of them a special quality.

With the approach of maturity, therefore, the hours become rarer and more precious. This is the critical period in our relation to time.

Either we give up, losing our footing and letting ourselves be swept along in the torrent, or we feel the moment has come to react, to go from heedless spending to jealous management.

At the age of eighty-five Pa Kin, the greatest poet of modern China, had just been decorated by President Mitterand and was invited to visit France. "To do what?" the poet asked, "To meet whom? To find what of interest?" "You realize," he added, as though to apologize for these questions, "my feeling is that I only have seven dollars left to my name—and I don't want to fritter them away on peanuts."

Although the need to avoid wasting time eventually becomes plain to all, few of us possess a suitable approach or method.

Before we can elaborate, we must understand how we learn time and how we then operate with this mysterious trinity of the past, present, and future.

Pediatricians have suggested that some twelve years go by before the child fully assimilates the mechanics of time. He generally learns to tell time before the age of eight. Then, he organizes in his mind the articulation of days, months, and years.

But these are mere codes, as different from inwardly perceived time as the reading of numbers on dollar bills is from having a sense of the value of money.

The important thing is to understand how our sense of time is formed and evolves. And, on this, few serious studies have been done. We note only that, as with affectivity and with moral values, the example set by our parents marks us in how we treat the hours.

Will we be punctual, because at home we saw an insistent respect for the hour, or will we refuse to follow a timetable, because we were too long subjected to supper at five-thirty on the dot? In either case, a backward look will prove fruitful. To recall how appointments were regarded at home, along with time allowed for completing a job or deadlines for projects, will help explain what has stayed with us or against which we have reacted.

Learning the constraints of time, at least the ones imposed from the outside, later derives from what is learned from school, family, . . . and television.

Obligatory schedules (including punishments or excuses), hour-long classes, changes in the program with the days of the week, waiting for weekends and vacation—all this dates back to school.

Waking up by oneself or at someone else's insistence, mealtimes, scurrying to get out of the house, reminders of work to be done, planning or lack of it for leisure and vacations is the legacy of the family. Added to them, of course, are the plans for the afternoon and evening with favorite and/or permitted TV programs.

This amalgam constitutes a quite substantial restraint. With the addition of some sports practice on Wednesday afternoon and one or two band rehearsals, our stressed Western children would have good reason to greet any rigid schedule with horror. Those children who conform to one with great zeal should even cause us some concern.

Just as a premature interest in theology yields future agnostics, the tyranny of the schedule wielded over children of ten runs the risk of their later rebelling against the least hint of personal organization.

We shouldn't exaggerate the danger, however, for human beings, especially the young, are remarkably adaptive. Don't they also get used to living amid bricks and asphalt and to seeing trees only as a rare pleasure?

More important is to gauge what the child is learning in this socialization by the clock. He will certainly know what others—society—demand of him in this area. He will have assimilated the appointments, the time allowed for projects, the chopping of the day into slices. But through lack of experience, he will not yet measure the exact dosage of these times.

At this stage, we may ask ourselves a question. Beginning in childhood, we have all faced schedules. We've all been encouraged to be punctual and been grumbled at for being late. How then does it happen that, ten or twenty years later, Jill arrives on time, completes her work on schedule, and appears relaxed, while Jack runs after the minutes, misses his plane, and always finds reasons for procrastinating?

Common sense suggests that there is an important difference between knowing what should be done and doing it.

This difference is often connected with a differing amount of motivation. Becoming a mathematician requires more than learning arithmetic. We have all learned the words of our language, but how many of us know how to write well?

In the mastery of time, an inequality of results is due only in part to differences in our innate abilities. The essence of the matter lies in an absence of instruction in this area. We are taught vocabulary (schedules) and spelling (respect for them), but we are not told how to construct clear, grammatical sentences. The message of the family and of society is a summary: "Manage for yourself! Manage to reconcile everything, meet the deadline—it is your problem!"

Furthermore, isn't this how we were taught a foreign language in school? With results that are well-known. No high school or college graduate speaks a foreign language fluently unless he or she has spent some time living where that language is spoken natively. For he or she lacks that dimension of actual experience that in time is inculcated by adult and professional life.

But we should not leave the time of childhood without mentioning a revealing fact. The beginning of our life is only incidentally the period when we learn the time of life in society.

It is in childhood that we are most profoundly, naturally, and intimately involved with time.

Never again will we be as open as the child, for whom all is new and who can dream, be surprised, forget all else to benefit from the moment. Without the burden of a past, without a care for the future, we experience our earliest years in the present, before our memories and plans gnaw it down from both ends.

The fundamental experience of the present, of the fullness of the moment, of the intensity of feeling (joy and misery; pleasure and suffering), the here and now, we acquire by instinct, easily.

This knowledge is decisive, for it is toward the recollection of it that we will later pursue. Mastering time has in fact two inseparable, although nearly opposite, goals. The most obvious, although not necessarily the most important, goal is to make better use of one's time. The most fulfilling—and the hardest— goal is to relearn to profit from the moment with the intensity we had at the age of seven as we came upon a shaft of sunlight in a pine woods.

Is this possible? Never completely. "You are neither the child you were," said the Buddhist sage Nagasema, "nor the old person you will become." A day in midvacation cannot have the same quality as one at the start. The conditions are too different. But the memory of what we previously felt at least enables us to enjoy what the day offers in the way of serene freedom.

The further we get from childhood, the more, in refining our knowledge of time, we modify our temporal horizon. This is one of the most significant and least-explored personal parameters.

The temporal horizon is the distance into the future or the past spontaneously reached by our mental vision, the duration explored by our attention. It varies quite a bit depending on the society, individual, and time of life.

Animals appear to have no temporal horizon. They live exclusively in the present, unable to call the past to mind (to re-experience a past moment, which is different

from recognizing a person, place, or event already encountered) or to anticipate (to imagine the future).

*We possess the faculty of making present use of our past
(what we learned or knew) to prepare for our future (foreseeing,
organizing, avoiding danger).*

In primitive societies the temporal horizon may extend
far back into the past but remains near in the opposite
direction, toward the future. Everything depends on
one's idea of time. To think about the future, we must
first believe in its existence. Primitive people thought of
time as circular and of the past as necessarily repeating
itself. It sufficed for them to predict the future by exploring the past and projecting it again up ahead of them.

Even today, many underdeveloped countries have a
too-near horizon with respect to the future. The famous
Latin American *mañana* means not only "tomorrow" but
just as likely "someday" or even "never." In the Middle
East, making an appointment more than a week ahead
runs the risk of never occurring because the local temporal horizon does not extend much beyond.

On the other hand, characteristic of Western civilization is the tilt of the temporal horizon toward the future
at the expense of the past. The Americans, with their
rather brief past, were the harbingers. It is they who
inculcated ancient Europe with planning, foresight,
scenarios for the future—without which there would
have been no Allied landing on the beaches of Nor-
mandy in June 1944, no landing on the moon in 1969.

We see the dangers of the reverse excess when children nowadays are saturated with rock music and don't

know which came first, the French Revolution or the American Revolution. But there can be more serious consequences to this approach. Obsessed with the days to come, especially rosy ones, the great "progressive" ideologies of the twentieth century preached that one could, in one blow, invert a people's temporal horizon. In the attempt to make a blank slate of the past, they have caused millions of deaths. Our century has slaughtered in the name of the future.

A better acquaintance with our own temporal horizon is of supreme importance if we want to master time. Do we belong with those people encumbered by memories like increasingly heavy baggage, or with those who complain of a failing memory? Do we painlessly look a month or a year ahead, or are we often surprised, looking at our calendar, at the appointments we've made for the next week?

We see very different temperaments and predispositions toward one or the other slope of the temporal horizon. In general, the past wins out over the future. Is this just because it takes less effort to remember than to foresee? Most of the disciplines connected with the mastery of time thus are about improving our relation to the near or distant future.

This is an imperative task, even though it conflicts with the legitimate desire to retrieve the intensity of the present. The aphorist Emile M. Cioran expresses it wonderfully well: "We can savor our days only if we shrug off the obligation to have a destiny."

Child, our horizon is very narrow. At the outset, we know only the present and thus know how to capitalize on it. But everything in our education later conspires to extend our horizon toward the future, through developing a respect for schedules, deadlines and examinations, and toward the past, since education involves memorization. To study is to form useful memories, from the multiplication table to human rights. We train for years in the central exercise of civilized man: to assimilate the past (the acquisition of the society we are born into) in order to be able to make use of it in the future.

The method is effective. When we are six years old, someone born three years before us seems old. At thirty, we begin to understand that an event that occurred a half century ago is almost recent.

Education pushes back the horizon toward the past. Professional life does the same for the future. We begin by solving problems from day to day. Then we quickly learn that to secure the most rewarding and hence most complex positions, we need to think further and further ahead. The horizon of a manager becomes his three-year plan, that of a writer his next book or books, that of an employee his vacation next year, the end of paying bills for his business, and then his retirement. The future pulls us forward.

Everything in our civilization leads us to the two limits of our temporal horizon. The present is merely a symbolic point through which our recollections move toward our expectations.

Westerners have forgotten the present. Bit by bit, they have whittled it down to nothing, and to retrieve it, they must undergo a genuine re-education.

This re-education, however, will not consist in erasing

the past and the future to reduce our horizon to the present. Among adults, only inmates in mental hospitals or nursing homes, isolated from everyone else, are permitted this return to childish unconcern.

On the contrary, for everyone else, including ourselves, only a firmer grasp of the past and future can restore the present to us. We can master a subject only through expertise. So we should first go further into punctuality, planning, and self-discipline, starting with the reverse of what we aspire to as our ultimate goal.

"What? Here I am struggling with all the forces that keep me from living, and you want me to add others?" The objection bursts out, almost automatically, before any attempt at mastery (of time, of one's body, of oneself).

Once again, the comparison with dietetics is instructive. People wanting to lose weight go on a diet because they do not feel good about themselves when they stand in front of a mirror. But they are overweight because every day they have opted for small, immediate gratifications (one more mouthful) over great satisfaction in the long run (looking and feeling good).

Now, dieting means doing without these little present and future gratifications while continuing to put up with the inconvenient corpulence that is not going to vanish right away. So one has to enter willingly an austere period with an eye to the likely benefits some time down the road.

This must be difficult, for failures are common. When we manage to do it, the situation had become truly intolerable, or we could keep up the effort by imagining the concrete benefits we would eventually obtain, or the required austerity brings other rewards (the woman in love begins losing weight because her sex life has become more rewarding than eating).

By mastering time, we go from a state of unwelcome tension to one of serenity and effectiveness.

Here, too, we must go through a period in which we are at first more constrained. But the good news is that the payoff comes much sooner than in dieting.

Two personal anecdotes illustrate the similarities between the two activities. After I'd taken off twenty-five pounds, I have had to smile when I heard: "Why are you dieting when you're so slim?" People seemed taken aback by the obviousness of my reply: "But it's *because* I'm dieting that I'm slim!" These are generally the same people who ask: "Where does a superorganized person like you find time for living?" and are incredulous when I answer: "It's only *since* I got organized that I have time for living."

Freedom is not found at the end of a gun, but in organization.

How, for example, can we improve our temporal horizon? By enriching it in two directions. To explore better our own past, for it contains the explanations of our current problems or blocks. This approach has been popularized by psychoanalysis, but we don't have to lie on a couch to do the exercise. We can learn a good deal from solitary, clear-headed retrospection.

Most of us still encounter our greatest problems in regard to the future, in the ability to anticipate. Like all

Westerners, we think in the future, but too often with anxiety or indecision. Hence the value of simple psychological techniques that will help make the future an ally. These will be described further on.

The problems we face concerning time include more than just depth of field. Not all of us have a simple appreciation of the time—the experience of duration—required to do things.

"Eternity is a long time—especially toward the end," said Woody Allen, with his genius for bringing out the obvious through the absurd. The certainty is that we cannot imagine eternity, nor even much less.

The age of the earth, for example, is more than four billion years. That is clearly a lot, but what difference is there for our brains between forty million or even four million?

So we should make up a metaphor, the way we do for children, translating this reality into a language we understand. Does one year mean something to you? Yes. Well, if the existence of the earth from its creation to the present was crunched into one year, humans would have made their first appearance only at a quarter to midnight on December 31, and Christ would have been born at 11:58 P.M. Now we have some concept of the age of the earth.

A millionth of a second—during which quite exciting things happen if one is an elementary particle—leaves us unimpressed. Are we even capable of appreciating the value of minutes?

Perceived duration is distorted by our emotions. What could be shorter than a night of lovemaking? What could be longer than the second our finger is caught in a car door? Depending on the interest we take in our work, a week goes by like a day or an hour may drag like a whole day.

Thus, only after much practice of various durations do we internalize the time needed to do things.

This seems simple, as our life is filled with repetitive activities. Nevertheless, in this area mature individuals persist in committing the errors of a beginner.

Thus, one of the leading doctors in Paris makes his patients spend between forty-five and ninety minutes sitting in his waiting-room. Every day. Sometimes, the delays reach such alarming proportions that his secretary has to call all of the afternoon patients to tell them to come in two hours later than originally scheduled.

The diagnosis is simple: the doctor books a patient every half hour, while he sees each for at least three-quarters of an hour. He's been doing this for years. And something in him refuses to recognize this.

How many times have we been collared by a coworker who asks if we've "got a minute?" and a half hour later is still going over his problem with us?

The simplest acts in life are not always timed in our head. A woman may in all sincerity claim she never needs more than ten minutes to put on her makeup (or a man to shave) although in fact she always takes twice as long.

It is neither common nor particularly pleasant to clock oneself, but nevertheless we need to know the respective durations of our daily activities. It is with these pieces of time that we construct our days. Several minor errors of evaluation piling up create long delays that end in the guilty telephone call: "Don't wait for me. Go ahead and start eating."

EXAMPLES OF DURATIONS

By the day	amounts to	By the year
5 minutes		30 hours
15 minutes		91 hours (4 days)
1 hour		15 days

In forty years, one hour a day adds up to 1.7 years.

Eight hours a night = four months a year of sleep.

We also, although less often, see the reverse behavior. People who allow too much time—showing up for appointments long in advance, filling waiting rooms, arriving at the airport hours before takeoff. These people are merely operating from different motives. Clearly, our attitude toward punctuality is not due to chance, and it works, as we shall see, as a mode of self-expression.

A well-known example: the systematic lateness of François Mitterand (at least before he became president and so was forced to abide by protocol). He appeared to need to keep people waiting. When in danger of being on time, he was seen to ask his chauffeur to pull off to the side of the road where he then proceeded to read a newspaper.

Thus, attitudes toward time vary quite a bit. Some people seem to have an internal clock and without a watch can always tell the exact time to within five minutes.

Others, however, live surrounded by timepieces but rarely glance at them and are forever surprised to hear it's much later or earlier than they thought.

Every one of us may usefully question himself and determine his posture with regard to the time required for some activity, punctuality, and a sense of what time it is. He will notice interesting parallels with the whole of his behavior in life.

We can already see that although time is unique, our perception of it is an individual matter that touches the very core of our personality.

But where the consequences are most significant for us, where we begin to encounter real problems, is in the way we use it. The lack of time has its source in our use of time.

THE USE OF TIME

◆

What we usually do • The day's appetizers
The need for locking up • Trying changes of rhythm
The brain on automatic pilot
The thirty-two time-stealers • The charms
of a lack of time • Avoiding sexuality
Five injunctions against time

The moment of truth comes about 5:00 P.M. Charles, who has been at the office since 8:00 this morning, tries to recall what he's done today. He's drawing a blank. For a full minute no exact memory comes to him. He isn't sick or drunk. It's the same nearly every evening.

He simply has trouble focusing on a treadmill day in which he was continually interrupted. How many times? He can't say; in fact, according to statistics, it must be about seventy-five times. And what is sitting on his desk is not a pleasing sight: two stacks of paperwork. In front, notes and the day's mail that he couldn't get to. Behind them, a still-unopened folder of material for the report he was supposed to write today.

He knows he still has thirty minutes of work to do if he wants to leave his secretary the letters she should type when she arrives in the morning. Then he'll head home with his papers under his arm, resigned to going over them after dinner.

When his wife sweetly asks what he's done at the office that day, he answers, "Nothing special"—and that is the truth.

This evening, he allows himself wine with dinner. His doctor has told him it's the best natural tranquilizer. He and his wife discuss the trip to Rome they may take next spring. Then he thinks again of his briefcase and doesn't have the heart for it. He watches a little TV, knowing he's liable to fall asleep in front of the set. Tomorrow, he swears, he'll get up at six, refreshed, to start his report while everyone is still asleep.

A commonplace scene repeated by the hundreds of thousands every day. Charles will end up getting his reports written, although not as soon or as well as he'd intended. But time will continue to slip through his fingers, for he doesn't have time to think about it.

We tend to consider ourselves victims, unable to find time in our lives. Yet, even if there are outside forces to contend with, we are not powerless to remedy the situation.

Through routine, a guilty conscience, or simply a lack of reflection, we unconsciously deprive ourselves of a large part of our time.

Let's look at a few of the many ways we do this.

Whether at work or at home, we have jobs to do. Small or big, it is these tasks that chop our days into pieces. But it is we who decide their order and who, in principle, determine their priority. In principle.

In fact we usually do:

What we enjoy doing before what we don't enjoy doing,

What goes quickly before what goes slowly,

What is easy before what is hard for us,

What is familiar before something new,

What others have imposed on us before what we have chosen ourselves.

That's not all. What we've penciled in for a given hour on our desk calendar takes precedence over work that is not assigned to any particular time. We tend to be more available for interrupters than for our own priorities. Similarly, we tend to deal with problems in the order in which they crop up—an order possibly unrelated to their importance.

When several parties depend on us, we deal first with the ones who are the most vocal in their demands, even when their problems are less than urgent. Isn't it the way we act with our clients or our own children?

Lastly, it is not surprising that these attitudes combine to get us launched on a task as late as possible and much too close to our deadline.

There's no need to emphasize that the above list, in which we can all recognize ourselves, points to what we should avoid if we want to make good use of our time. But these attitudes are the ones that have been natural to us since our school days and that we have had little occasion to change, except perhaps for the worse, under the pressure of professional duties.

There is, of course, the law of least effort.

Let's face it: inside many a workaholic lurks a lazy child with his own instinctive method for dodging additional work while giving the impression (even to himself) of doing tons of it!

The sociofamilial defense for a ten- to twelve-hour work day establishes an solid cover for you. No one would dare to take a peek at what is actually going on inside. The height of chic (or rudeness) was discovered by the noted advertising man who is the last to arrive at dinners at his own home. He further increases his value in his own eyes by choosing to look more overworked than urbane.

Even though we may all have our share of some secret lackadaisicalness, this cannot be the whole explanation. Modern industrial societies were not created by a bunch of goof-offs. Other psychological mechanisms must be involved.

Many of us find it hard to get into their work in the morning, to get back into the necessary rhythm. We allow ourselves a transitional period, getting started with little chores that are not too long or too hard: making a phone call or two, reading a couple of letters no longer than two pages. After which, we swear, we'll tackle the big jobs.

The bother is that before we've polished off the appetizers, the others attack. With telephone calls, interruptions, letters (the mail's delivered), they throw us balls that we are, like a well-trained seal, deft at catching gracefully on the tips of our noses. And things are set in motion for the rest of the day: we'll play sea lions until dark.

No sooner do we get warmed up to our task, the slicing of the hours into minutes is resumed by the interrupters who come sabotaging the brief space of time in which we could have made some sustained effort. Fortunately, it does happen that we are left in peace. With a little time freed up, we are finally, we swear, going to be able to get some work done.

A day full of activity, even intense activity, saps our energy, wears on our nerves, but makes little demands on our brains. Most everyday work contains little that is novel. Creativity, originality, the capacity for innovation—anything that stimulates our brain power—is nearly precluded at the outset. We have merely to see the consideration and monetary rewards that creative people receive to conclude that their qualities are uncommon.

The rest of us can handle most situations using an average stock of ideas, an adequate store of experiences, and a bit of common sense.

Of all the parts that go to make us up, it is the brain that is by far the most underemployed.

We must make more intensive use of it in writing, thinking, calculating, and planning than we do for discussing, telephoning, dictating, taking part in meetings, and even, too often, making decisions.

Switching from routine thinking to genuine concentration is like jumping from a slow moving-sidewalk to a faster one. We have to mobilize our energy and flexibility before jumping. And we have no great liking for these changes of rhythm.

Spending a day carved up into various undemanding tasks, we prefer to continue in the same mode. If we are deep into work requiring sustained thought, but need to take an hour to make some phone calls, we will subsequently find it hard to pick up the thread of our thinking.

These changes in rhythm are trying because our brain is a biological, not electronic, machine. Getting it started and changing gears takes more than pressing a button. The brain needs plateaus, adaptation time, hysteresis.

Now, the fractionation of modern time and the proliferation of our activities have forced us to abbreviate these pauses, downgearing them until they are totally eliminated. Appointments, meetings, and telephone calls are chained together with no transition.

Most of our work we do on automatic pilot. This represents progress in an airplane but not in us.

Only individuals like salespeople, who must travel between appointments, have a chance to reflect on what they have just experienced and prepare themselves for the next stage.

"The man or woman in the technological society has suppressed the natural respites in their rhythm," concluded French philosopher Jacques Ellul. "The time for choosing, adapting, and collecting oneself no longer exists. The rule of life has become: 'No sooner said than done.'"

We are impelled to skip from one kind of activity to another with no intervening space to get some impetus. Thus, we often do not jump, and instinctively remain in the same register.

Neither altogether lazy nor truly superficial nor hopelessly stupid, we all are liable to such dissipation of our time. It is enough for these tendencies to exist and show up regularly to throw all of our time out of kilter.

The way in which we set our priorities, choose where to begin, and shift our rhythm does not constitute the whole problem. Studies have been done for decades to determine lists of these *time stealers* that we encounter just about every day. They seem to be everywhere the same.

In the early 1970s the sociologist Alec MacKenzie had various executives draw up lists of time stealers. He interviewed forty Canadian army colonels, thirty American university presidents, twenty-five Mexican company heads, insurance brokers, black clergymen, and German managers. MacKenzie found that their lists were virtually interchangeable. The full complement of thieves includes the following:

External thieves
Unexpected and prolonged phone calls,
Coworkers stopping by to discuss their problems or to chat,
Open door politics, the duty to be available,
Visitors, clients, unexpected suppliers,

Poorly trained or incompetent personnel (particularly, inadequate secretarial help),

The boss or, worse, several bosses,

Business lunches, promotional cocktail parties, and other entertainment for outside visitors,

Personal or family business,

Maintenance, machine repairs (cars, washing machines, television),

Appointments (doctor's, music lessons, sports) for the children and chauffeuring them,

Housework, errands, cooking,

Interruptions by one's children (or one's parents).

Internal thieves

Confused and changeable objectives and priorities,

Absence of a daily work plan,

No self-imposed deadlines,

Tendency to do too much, perfectionism,

Lack of order, messy desktops,

Confusion and overlap of responsibilities,

Insufficient delegation,

Excessive attention to details,

Delay in dealing with conflicts,

Resistance to change,

Scattered or too-numerous interests,

Inability to say no,

Lack of information, insufficient (or excessive) communication,

Indecisiveness or overhasty decisions (or decisions made in committee),

Fatigue, being out of shape.

It would be pointless to give specific examples. Reading this list of thirty-two time stealers, every reader can remember cases in his or her own personal experience. Then begins the debate about whether external or internal factors steal more time.

The management expert Peter Drucker performed an illuminating experiment. A film he's made showed a company president committing in the course of a day just about every crime imaginable against the good use of his time and that of his employees.

He asked forty supervisors to make their own list of time stealers before they watched the film. Most of them blamed external factors. Then he asked them to revise their lists after seeing the film. The vast preponderance of time stealers became internal.

If we are honest with ourselves as we reread this list of external time stealers, we will realize that many of them are merely internal ones in disguise. In essence they are the handmaidens of two internal time stealers: "an inability to say no," which leaves one swamped with visits, needless and overlong telephone calls, trivial errands, fatigue, nonessential tasks, so-called obligations, and insufficient delegation, which prevents us from sparing ourselves a host of professional or family chores that could be done by others or organized differently.

So, how should we organize ourselves around the unpredictable? Certainly, not all constraints are spurious. There are emergencies (but few real ones, a doctor friend often reminds me). In principle, our bosses have the right to interrupt us whenever they like.

If this were strictly true, no secretary could master his or her time. Many of them succeed in doing so, however, because they have succeeded in training their bosses.

All these findings add up to both good news and bad news. The bad news is that there is almost nobody around us to blame. The good news is that we do have the power to make changes and that we can even enjoy considerable room to maneuver.

Our progress seems to have led us to a door we will have to open: our own. Like the needle of a compass pointing to the north, the needle of time, whatever detours we take, points inevitably toward us, with whom the problem starts and ends.

Certainly, the social time we live in makes life complicated. The behavior of others is frequently of little help. We would be right to sue our society and our peers for the erosion of our time capital. But would we have any chance of winning the case?

These facts are as unyielding as time. We will not change them, although we can to some degree accommodate ourselves to them, even turn them to our benefit. Let us recall (not for the last time) two self-evident truths:

Time passes without stopping. Although we can lose time, we cannot gain time. All we can do is make better use of the time we have.

From start to finish, to master one's time is to gain mastery of oneself.

We begin life with the instinctive and self-protective idea that adversity always comes from the outside. "It's not me, it's him," all children cry. Forty years later, some of us are still crying the same thing.

But the security coming from the fact of having lived and overcome certain obstacles sometimes gives us (is this maturity?) an intimation of a more efficacious truth: *The enemy is within us—therefore the toughest one to over-power, as we usually treat ourselves with leniency.*

Before making a deft and methodical attack on the self, we should examine the reasons for its weaknesses. Each of us will do the examining in his or her own way, but the observation of some common cases may prompt some ideas and permit comparisons.

If we go on tolerating a situation like the shortage of time, even though we never cease loudly complaining about it, may it not well be true that some aspects of it suit us?

Observe someone who is chronically late. There he is finally coming to the meeting where everyone else is already seated. He enters, noisily apologizes, disturbs a whole row taking his place, spreads out his things, apologizes again, and sometime dares in all seriousness to add: "Please go on, don't pay me any mind."

He fills the house with his shouts—"Has anyone seen my brown shoes?"—and mobilizes his whole entourage who fear he will miss his plane.

There have been rewards for these games. For example, attracting attention, getting oneself noticed. Instead of establishing his worth by his mighty feats or achievements, he opts for negative attention—"What a pest!"—over none at all. In the face of his or her parents' indifference, the child instinctively knows what bit of misbehavior will assuredly get the spotlight back.

The habitual laggard is also creating some excitement, an artificial anxiety that he or she prefers to the absence of stimulation. When life seems dull, one may treat oneself to a few thrills by playing at "Am I going to miss my plane?" (and forget my toothbrush?).

Lastly, by making other people wait, the least prominent member of a group can enjoy a brief sense of controlling it. By preventing others from starting—to leave, or to speak, or to eat—when they want to, he displays in his own eyes a bit of the power he fears he lacks.

If punctuality is the courtesy of kings, tardiness may be the sport of the unhappy.

The overworked individual may also have unspoken reasons for resisting any perceptible improvement in the situation he complains about.

Traditionally, men have used job responsibilities to get out of doing most household chores. And it still works. It also may be a long-standing pretext to avoid having to explore the expectations of his own children.

At the office, the overworked individual presents a furrowed brow to any problem he finds unpleasant to deal with. If he never has the time to take the problem up, he hopes it will go away by taking care of itself. After all, in one-third of most cases, that is what in fact happens. More or less satisfactorily.

Supervisors, who have a holy terror of confrontations with their employees, also work this way. They never find the time to explain to them what won't do. Similarly, politicians who can't bear to concern themselves in the financing of their activities will always have more urgent things to deal with, all the while counting on a miracle.

Things the overworked individual may be seeking to avoid include responsibility, intimacy, and well-being.

Responsibility is never far from guilt. As soon as we show the slightest aptitude for solving problems, everyone (superiors, coworkers, subordinates, spouses, children, friends) seem to vie with each other in proposing new ones for us. One after another, obligations grab onto our backs like baby opossums.

To preserve our vital space time, we must be able to refuse without wounding. The alibi works well in two ways that each of us uses according to his temperament: the "I can't" or the "I don't know."

The "I can't" is the prerogative of strong and believable persons who we readily concede are already doing a lot. It is the audible sigh, the eyes turned to heaven, a few words that make clear in advance that in this case our hero is at the end of his or her tether and that it would be ungracious to insist.

The "I don't know" is preferred by people who find it more indisputable to plead conclusive ineptitude. Their balance sheet of time mastery is so plainly disastrous, their delays, their omissions, their forgetfulness so manifest and recurrent that truly no one would be so foolish as to entrust them with the slightest responsibility. This strategy is not ego building, but it is highly effective.

The lack of time also constitutes a convenient stronghold for avoiding others and warding off intimacy. For some persons, two elements in the life of a couple become threatening over time: sexuality and communication. They no longer feel able to respond to the wishes of the other, or for various reasons simply have little desire to do so.

For sexuality, the overworked life may be a cause as well as pretext. The decline in libido of overworked management is the daily bread of sexologists.

In any event, the office where the lights are on very late often shelters someone who has found good reasons for not going home. And when he does, his "tension" will justify his hardly saying a thing during supper and then his going to bed as soon after that as he can.

This technique is effective. This way, a couple may avoid touching any sensitive subject for years on end— providing they hold out that long.

Finally, resistance to the mastery of time may feed on the fear of well-being. People suffering from something all speak of getting rid of it. But if the opportunity arises, not all seize it. That would be too simple.

The state of guilt inherent in our Judeo-Christian morality leads some of us to believe that a portion of misery in life guarantees against worse yet. If everything began going better, fate might avenge itself by striking harder. Hamlet soliloquizes about the dread of "The undiscovered country ... [that] makes us rather bear those ills we have/ Than fly to others we know not of."

And then, time etches our features, digs lines in our brows, and the person who slipped into the skin of the busy character is not always ready to shed it. How could he replace it? Should he find another definition of himself? When choice is offered between a stressful life and asking fundamental questions about oneself and the meaning of life, the answer is not obvious.

This often unconscious guilt is intimately mingled with our relation to time. We cannot analyze, understand, and do something about this relation unless we manage to identify these messages internalized in childhood.

Often, we act as though it is legitimate to take time for ourselves only when we have satisfied all the demands of others—in other words, never.

Sometimes, we are so imbued with this that we instinctively class as spineless laxity every moment not devoted to pure action. Hence an observable distrust of preliminary reflection, a period of recuperation, creative reverie, relaxation, the acquisition of knowledge that is not immediately useful.

These overabbreviated moral precepts should be treated according to Talleyrand's advice: "Always rely on principles. They will end up yielding." For though they were valuable in building our character, the moment always arrives when they thwart our development.

A psychologist, Kahler, selected the five commonest injunctions that have affected our attitude toward action: Hurry, Be perfect, Please me, Try again, Be strong. Each of these attitudes has certain pernicious effects.

The *hurry up*s believe that if one can accomplish something by taking one's time, it must not be very important or serious. They require great haste in order to feel justified. So for them, it's quite normal to set about doing something at the last minute.

The *be perfect*s do not know when to stop adjusting the last details. They lose time tidying, refining, checking, securing. They have trouble making decisions, for they are afraid they are missing some crucial information. Their perfectionism slows them down and prevents them from taking a detached look at what they are doing.

The *please me*s often say yes when they are thinking no and find themselves committed to a number of activities that they dislike. They don't like to be the bearers of bad news, which leads them to inaction about situations that are getting worse. They dare not disclose their goals or intentions.

The *try again*s think that "it" has to be hard and difficult. If it isn't, they don't take the problem seriously. They concentrate more on the effort than on the results. For them, rather than finishing up, it is more important to know that they have spared nothing . . . and gotten hardly any sleep.

The *be strong*s don't need anyone else. They have to find solutions by themselves and don't know how to delegate. They confess to no weakness and they don't complain. They take on everything themselves and have trouble admitting their mistakes.

These behaviors are clearly the result of programming by our parents and teachers. But we aren't always aware of them. They have become instincts that are expressed when our reflection and rationality are not fully under control. Now, who can believe that they are fully under control all the time, expecially during days of tension?

These situations do not apply (and never all together) to everyone. They represent examples of the infinite variety of inner obstacles standing in the way of the good use of our time. Each of us may fill this zoo with his own specimens.

When we add the traps of personal time to the constraints of modern time, do we need to insist on the necessity, urgency, and difficulty of the mastery of time?

THE MASTERY OF TIME

Confronted with inalterable, irreversible, and indifferent time, the paltry creatures that we are dare to dream of mastering it. Is this madness or an absurd pretension?

Is mastering time like the cowboy riding a mustang after he's been thrown a dozen times? Not at all. In a rodeo, the trick is the balance between the horse's power and the rider's tenacity. Against time, not only are we not the stronger, but we have no hold over it at all. No more than we have over our need at every moment in life to breathe in oxygen.

Thus, what for convenience (or boasting?) we call the mastery of time may mean merely the mastery of ourselves with regard to time. The horse we are riding will not stop or slow down. There is no question of cutting the reins. Here we seek the means of not letting ourselves be dragged on the ground or of not tossing about, but also of righting ourselves, of beginning to ride to its pace, sometimes even of managing to outstrip it.

Are we capable of mastery, and do we know what it is? Consider an example of mastery that most of us have: the ability to drive a car.

There was a time when, having never put our hands to the steering wheel, we were both eager and fearful. Not yet knowing much about it, we wondered how one could casually drive a car at more than eighty miles an hour while chatting pleasantly or thinking about something completely unrelated.

After a few lessons came the day when we were convinced that we would never manage to let the clutch out, engage the right gear, use the turn signal, and glance at the rear-view mirror before making a turn, all at the same time.

Then the day finally arrived when we casually drove the car over eighty miles an hour, chatting all the while. But that day, we weren't even thinking about it. We'd gained mastery of driving.

People who are fluent in a foreign language know that the process is the same. Phase 1: one has no ideas about the language and the goal of speaking it and the result seems as unreachable as it is desirable. Phase 2: the start of the training confirms our worst fears. Phase 3: through sustained effort we manage to practice the language without thinking about the fact that we are speaking it, only about what we are going to say.

Achieving mastery of a new activity proceeds in three stages: the motivation that makes us want the results; the will that enables us to overcome our initial disorientation and discouragement; finally, the completed internalization, where we are no longer concentrating on the mastery itself, which has now been learned, but on what, thanks to it, we can achieve.

But what is a master and what can we expect of mastery?

In one of Michel Random's films about the martial arts in Japan, we see the master Ueshiba practicing Aikido. For many minutes, the smiling little man of seventy-five is set upon by husky young men, advanced students, who in turn or all together try to throw him; he, content to agitate his arms a bit, outlines some feints, throws them literally off in the distance. A small effort, large effects.

Another image of mastery: in the film *From Mao to Mozart*, violinist Isaac Stern demonstrates proper bowing technique to an audience of diligent Chinese musicians. Relaxed and making jokes with his interlocutors, Stern draws forth from his instrument harmonies that bring tears to one's eyes.

Again a master: the surgeon who was asked how in his small and modestly equipped hospital he got the best results in asepsis and cicatrization in the whole city: "I know just where to make the incision."

Precision, economy of means, and the near absence of effort: mastery is the sister of elegance.

An elegant solution or a mathematical proof joins ingenuity with simplicity. One doesn't need to be a master to understand the process of gaining mastery. We have all had occasion to take up new sports or professional activities where, by dint of repetition, we ended up by cutting the time we initially needed by half or more. And with much less fatigue.

Through mastery—thanks to knowledge, practice, and especially the confidence gained in our ability to find solutions—we understand how to dominate a problem that had hitherto dominated us.

Practiced and self-assured, we finally succeed in doing what is the very essence of mastery: applying our energy at the right spot. We will see that this is one of our richest sources of inner satisfaction.

So what is it to be master of one's time, if not knowing how to fit into it, moving in it, relying on it, protecting oneself with it, using it, and taking pleasure in it? It does not move, we live in it, giving it form through our acts and movements. "The use of time," says philosopher Lucien Sève, "is the real infrastructure of the developed personality."

Economist Jacques Lesourne identifies it in an attractive formula: "The web in which I am both the spider and the fly." In fact, we can imprison ourselves by the way we spin out our time. Eventually we will learn to spin this web to suit our expectations of time and of life in general.

For whatever we do, time weaves a pattern every day. It is just a matter of influencing the design to suit us and only occasionally producing a sense of letting ourselves be tied down.

• The doctor who treats us as though we were the day's only patient. He or she listens attentively and never checks the clock. Yet we know his or her waiting room is crowded with patients who will be seen after us.

• The friend living in a foreign capital whom we phone on our arrival there and who receives us instantly, hosts us for an evening, and drives us back to the airport. We secretly think that if he had done as we had, he would have upset our plans and irritated us by not telephoning or writing ahead.

• The mother (ours?) who is always there for her children and fixes marvelous dinners, makes herself beautiful for her husband, and radiates great good humor.

• The married woman with an absorbing career, and part of a healthy couple, who lets not a day go by without crossing town to visit her ailing father in the hospital.

• The boss who never makes you wait more than a day after your request to see him or her. He or she never takes refuge behind a schedule that you know is extremely tight, and then speaks to you without the least tension.

• Any person who leads a varied life (professional, personal, cultural, physical) with no apparent sacrifice.

To unfailing serenity, availability to others and multiple interests, the true masters of time, thanks to their detachment, will add humor.

But since mastering time concerns ourselves and not others, these appearances tell us little about what approach to take. In fact, the approach is marked out with beacons: a certain number of insights are preliminary to making any progress and these insights concern what we all to some degree lack before we bring about the transformation.

The obstacle to mastery is, as we have already mentioned, primarily in ourselves. These are deficiencies in us that fall into one or more of the following four categories:

1. *We do not know ourselves well enough.*
2. *We do not understand time well enough.*
3. *We let ourselves be harried by ourselves and by others.*
4. *We do not reflect enough about our use of time.*

1. "No wind can be favorable," declared the sixteenth-century Dutch prince William of Orange, "for one who knows not where he's going." Nor is mastery possible for one who does not know himself. But, a great part of what we are and what we want remains fuzzy, even for us.

Sometimes we have a clear and simple awareness of what we want, sometimes we have merely vague and poorly connected impressions, as if we preferred seeing just the tip of the iceberg and leaving the rest submerged in the unconscious.

We can take control of our time only if we know what we want to do with it: generally and specifically, in the final analysis or in stages—a fundamental process discussed in the next chapter.

No one knows the limits of our self-confidence better than we do. No one has suffered more from our inadequacies, has fallen more often into the traps that we ourselves have set, or has disappointed us more often than we ourselves.

We all have our lapses and tendencies to drift off-course. Mastery demands that we cope with them and begin by drawing up a not too indulgent inventory of ourselves.

2. Understanding time better and becoming watchful observers show how our experienced time fits in with society's time. Most of our stresses and slippages come from a poor fit between the two. Mistaken notions about how long things take or the time available for them are the sources of all overwork and disappointments.

A close look at what actually happens as our days unfold (including, if need be, measuring it in hours and minutes) is part of the information to acquire or to make more precise. This information helps us realize that any arbitrary cutting up of our time—for example, between professional and personal time— prevents us from mastering it.

The mastery of time is not a sporadic attitude. Either it applies to the full twenty-four hours in a day or it is just a put-on, like dieting at lunch but not at dinner.

3. Insight into what is needlessly cluttering up our time is as critical as it is down to earth. It comes from doing one's housework.

In every room and on every desk sit objects, leftover papers, and never-used dust-catchers that we have forgotten there because we see them all the time. One day, it occurs to us to take a fresh look at everything, and in a few moments the stuff vanishes without regret into the trash basket or attic. Similarly, our time is littered with routines or chores to be eliminated.

Because these time clutterers may be less easily spotted, we will look in detail at how to identify them so as to get rid of them. Here, we need merely note that they have three sources: other people, ourselves, and, more particularly, our memory.

Other people create an impressive list of yeses that should have been nos (not always owing to weakness or goodness, but often simply from lack of thought), adding up to hours and even days sacrificed to no purpose.

From ourselves, we use up time with all the gestures we make through habit, like, for example, tidying, maintenance, cleaning something every day when once or twice a week would be quite sufficient.

But a quite special place should be made for the clearing away of memory. Trying to remember everything is as ambitious and pointless as climbing five flights of stairs instead of taking the elevator—good physical exercise, but not necessarily good common sense when carrying grocery bags.

What we commit ourselves to holding in memory limits a part of our mental availability to the passive role of merely storing ideas; on the other hand, what we happen to forget produces frustrating disturbances in our temporal development.

Each of us has worked up a practical system of keeping memories (such as keeping a diary), but few that prove reliable enough for us to relax enough to then empty out the emotional or mental storage space in an attempt to convert it to more creative purposes.

4. Finally, by admitting that the three insights thus described are on the right track, we will have certainly cleared the ground, but we have yet to put a plan into action.

Hence the need for a motor for advancing beyond reflection and concentration. For all knowledge or insight is academic when not translated into action.

Mastery is not just a piece of knowledge or an attitude, but a practical experience that can be put to work only through concentrating on the use of our time—hourly, daily, weekly, monthly, annually, and existentially.

These four components of mastery suggest that the master of one's time has internalized some key notions:

He knows at every instant what he wants to use his time for.

He knows his failings and weaknesses and has learned to outsmart them.

He has developed his instinct and experience of the time required for every act or phase of his life.

He lives just one (professional or personal, routine or unusual) time: his own.

He frees his memory of the "what" in favor of the "how" and the "why"; he has memory aids that help him forget nothing.

He focuses his thought each day on the use of his time in relation to his goals.

It is certainly not enough to write down or even to memorize these abilities. Only to the strongly motivated can we propose sustained efforts and suggest practical stages in these directions. That will be the topic of the remainder of this book.

First, motivation, for we will not take on a project like this without inspiring ourselves with a clear vision of the ensuing benefits. The mastery of time is more than a weapon against stress.

The linguist and philosopher Caleb Gattegno says that "To live is to change time into experience." He adds that it is important that this transaction should be as satisfying as possible.

We all recognize that along with health, time is our only true wealth, the coin against which we obtain successive impressions of life. Not paying too much, not spending foolishly, not squandering our irreplaceable capital: when applied to life, these administrative notions become less abstract.

We realize that in relation to time, money is nothing. When justice wants to punish, the fine and the foreclosure are mere peccadilloes. We dread only the punishments that deprive us of our time of freedom. The most barbaric of them, the death penalty, is the one that in one blow annihilates all the time that remains.

Because time is the very warp and woof of life, the mastery of time assumes the very highest priority. Who would deliberately accept wasting one's life, or even a little of it?

Furthermore, making good use of our time is a major satisfaction whose effects are known to all. The Roman emperor Titus, builder of the Coliseum, is said to have asked himself each evening: "Have I made good use of my time today?" Those of us who do so have a sense of accomplishment when their day has unfolded harmoniously, without squandering, consistent with our goals and expectations. And even more so if they were aware of this at every moment.

On the other hand, we experience chagrin each evening when, in response to the same question, we relive all the unproductive waiting, the perpetual interruptions, the deadlines not met, rushing so much we feel as battered as if we had tumbled down a hill.

The first goal of mastery is to avoid the sense that time is tightening like a rope around your neck. To be sure, we should not confuse control and mastery. We can certainly benefit from "managing" time, which enables us to fit in more tasks in the same amount of time. This is progress, but it does not change life.

Controlling and managing our time brings about a better-coordinated sequence of activities but does not ensure the essential thing—namely, a vision of the whole, even of meaning.

How does the mastery of time bestow this vision? Thanks to several attitudes that come into play before, during, and after the action, and these will be discussed further on.

But we may already reflect for a moment on this crucial point: the very meaning of the mastery of time is to optimize its *quality* and only derivatively its amount and effectiveness. We cannot confine ourselves just to accomplishing more in the same amount of time or less.

For some people, doing a thing well matters as much or more than doing it at all. These are the ones who are best prepared for realizing that mastery brings its own rewards, for along with the desired result comes the pleasurable experience of achieving it in one of the best possible ways.

Here we find a subtle but important stimulus to seek to master time, which appears in a double dimension: in the first degree, achieving mastery in order to obtain better concrete results; at the second (perhaps primordial) degree, achieving mastery in order to enjoy a sense of know-how, of dominating a situation, and of learning a new competency.

For some people, the ultimate goal may be less the knowledge that they have mastered their time than their possession of this mastery. But a person currently struggling with an overcrowded schedule may be satisfied with less. He may wonder whether we are not falling prey to unnecessary complications.

Let us be content to note that today we cannot mention mastery without referring schematically to two principles of millennia-old Eastern wisdom that are worth reviving in our own day:

"The goal matters less than the path by which we reach it," or again: the result is less important than the means we use to obtain it. This is the opposite of saying "the end justifies the means."

We dominate only the thing from which we have stood at some distance." This is more applicable every day. What lives inside us obsesses us and has a hold on us. As long as we do not detach ourselves from it somewhat, we are susceptible to rage, passion, or simple annoyance. To overcome our rage, we must be able to say: "I am feeling a rage, but I am not this rage; therefore I can just as well not feel it later."

We need this distancing, this de-identifying with something that is causing a problem so that we can consider the difficulty or task from the outside and distinguish its elements with equanimity.

Achieving detachment is prerequisite to any mastery: to make progress, we must observe and judge what we are doing while we are doing it.

This is both exceedingly simple (it is enough to think of it and to have the time for it) and, in our unstudied behavior, fairly infrequent. We have seen how the modern fractionating and compression of modern time has eliminated this indispensable mental lubricant from our life.

It is also through the quest for distance that we hope to bring about our rediscovery of the present.

When the painter stands back from her canvas or the sculptor from his statue, he or she physically distances himself from the object. In pure thought, the corresponding process involves "becoming conscious of . . ." what is going on, of what we have just said or of what we are thinking.

Because our brain can focus on only one thing at a time, however, we do not manage—except in a flash—to think or act at the same time as we are conscious of doing it. When we must (for lack of time?) choose between the two, most often we prefer (since we are not dreamers) thinking/acting rather than "being conscious of."

Now, as we have seen, thinking or acting typically consists in using the past to prepare for the future. This involves creating products (thoughts or actions) from raw materials (knowledge and experiences). Absorbed in the exercise and pressured by the need to repeat it, we fail to become conscious of what we are doing, of looking at ourselves and feeling. And that is how we bypass the present.

In the course of our daily actions and thoughts, becoming conscious of what we are doing is to rediscover the present.

It is impossible to remain permanently in the present like, say, a cat. Only contemplatives can manage this, and that only when they are contemplating; when they are fixing their dinner, they have the same problems we do.

Thus, at best, our present comes to us fragmented by repeated comings to consciousness in the unfolding of our activity.

This involves a sort of mental dance in which, as we shift our weight from one foot to the other, we nimbly shift our minds in relation to what absorbs us, seeing it, appreciating it, feeling it in full awareness. Then we come back to it, having registered an impression of the present.

Thus, when I am talking to someone, for an instant my mind leaves the ideas exchanged and regards itself speaking. At that moment it may think: "This is dragging, I must be more assertive . . . nice weather . . . his tie is horrible." Then back into the discussion.

So it is the same process of coming to consciousness that allows us to achieve mastery and to reintroduce the fleeting present.

Its value, however, goes beyond this. If we go one step further, we may modify our attitude toward change.

Isn't it precisely change that enables us to note the existence of time? Change is time made concrete. But we lack a confident relationship with it. Once we are grown up, the physical changes in store for us seem to be for the worse; as for psychological changes, we have a poor grasp of them and we distrust their effects.

Starting with this observation, journalist Gail Sheehy investigated the "predictable crises of adults." She relied on academic research to cast doubt on the traditional notion that between youth and old age—two periods of intense change—adult life forms a relatively stable plateau.

Describing ten-year periods—of which, five often involve a crisis of adaptation followed by five of calmer waters—Sheehy confirmed what many a person over forty has often suspected: the path of our lives is more like a twisty mountain road than a straight flat interstate across the plains.

In this connection, who of us over forty foresaw or even felt his or her midlife crisis coming on? Why couldn't we anticipate it, even defuse it? That would require information (knowing that it is likely and hence normal), confidence (thinking something can be done about it), and standing back (enabling to observe and interpret the advance signals in ourselves).

Is anticipating changes in ourselves the final stage in mastering time? No, better still, desiring these changes. Starting from the moment we stop being afraid of changes, we understand that they present us with genuine opportunities for living in the present.

Couples are advised to combat sexual boredom by getting a change of scene before they set about changing partners. Here we are dealing with the use of change to gain a new appreciation of the present. And what could be more "in the present" than the act of love?

Similarly, an unexpected event brings us back to the present, and not always pleasantly so. When the pilot announces that the plane will be taking off two hours late, he immediately sets off an instant of consciousness on the theme of "what am I doing here?"

Our desire for novelty, the unexpected, breaking routine, plays the same role as a cold shower. We desire these small or large changes for they help us meet up anew with the present.

We can imagine different images of the master of his time. He or she may be that impeccable programmer, experienced calculator, meticulous organizer who is not surprised or unsettled by anything unexpected. That would already be good.

But I like him or her better with the features of the attentive and smiling thinker who is mentally dancing from one moment to the next. He or she is a good judge of himself and of reality, has a keen sense of the passing moment, knows how to take advantage of it (and may also suffer from it), but adapts to it very quickly. This person knows how to alternate periods of intensity and dreaminess, for he or she knows the value of change. Change is his element and helps him to exist, for he has overcome his fear of it. Everyone is surprised at her availability; some even wonder if she is not under-employed. She knows this and enjoys a laugh about it. For him or her time is flexible.

You can invent a wholly different character to suit yourself—a model that will be useful to buoy your spirits on a voyage that will sometimes be rough.

For the real world rarely permits complete mastery. It is useful to describe it, as a horizon, a reference point. But in our daily lives, constraints remain in force.

To master our time, we have a sense that we first need to be masters of ourselves, without a boss, without subordinates, even without a family. But who can afford to start one's life from scratch?

Hence the objection: "All this is of concern only to a few privileged characters. It doesn't apply to my case."

But suppose this is an excuse for not even trying? None of our lives is ideal, so we all can stand to make some progress. A little? A lot? Totally? That will depend less on the individual's specific circumstances than on the energy that he or she is willing and ready to put into the transformation.

We come back, as always, to motivation, which in the modern world is "the main force of armies," much more so than discipline. So it is time to explore how we can find it in ourselves to make these changes and, above all, to preserve it.

THE TIME FOR PROJECTS

◆

Going faster than time • What do we do now?
The need for meaning and progress
The priority of pleasure • Our fields of work
The fifteen times of life • Inadmissible projects
A method for helping the dream • Your last six months
The secret of top performances

At the starting line of the Olympic slalom, the contestants are waiting for the race to get under way. Silent, helmets and goggles hiding their faces, their eyes closed, the skiers *look at* the trail where everything will be played out in less than two minutes. Their arms folded in front of them, their right hands make twisting motions, like the turns they themselves will make around the poles.

Just before taking off down the slope, these expert skiers mentally go over the whole trail. They run through the circuit they are to follow without any chance to reflect. This preparatory concentration is required for them to perform at their peak.

The night before a delicate negotiation, a speech to give, or a test to take, each of us has done this kind of mental recapitulation of the arguments, the essential points, the potential traps.

When we enter a critical or hazardous period in life, we feel the need not to face the totally unknown, and in our imaginations we simulate what is awaiting us.

Unfortunately, all too often what should be productive concentration turns to anxiety. And we generally reserve this effort for exceptional occasions even though it could be a valuable tool in our daily work.

For though we can do nothing about the passing of time, we do have a major trump card: thanks to our brain, we can go faster than time.

We can, if not with certainty, then at least with probability, know therefore in advance where time is taking us to. It is our lone trump card, but a considerable one. The art of time consists in playing it to the fullest advantage.

Overtaking time in thought involves three distinct abilities: *prediction* (In a month I'll be leaving for Hawaii); *volition* (I want to take up surfing while I'm there); getting ready (I'm not in shape, but before I go I'll practice balancing with a skateboard).

In modern societies, all of us are obliged to make predictions. If we do not, there'll be no seat on the plane, no money toward the end of the month, no food in the refrigerator for supper. This not-very-original programming, which at the minimum involves the use of a calendar, has been to some degree accomplished by all. Prediction is within everyone's grasp and makes life more pleasant.

Volition or wanting is generally formulated much less clearly. We think we know what we want, but on closer inspection, the vagueness of our desires outweighs their precision.

Preparation, which should be the logical outcome of

predicting and wanting, is the prerogative of only a minority of us. There's nothing surprising about this, for these are the active, efficacious few.

It is worth taking a closer look at our wondrous power to make plans (which must be desired and prepared for) and the very limited use we make of it. All regaining control of our time begins with this obligatory step.

Strangely, at a time when we are presented with opportunities for choice that were unknown to earlier generations, and in the free countries we happen to live in, it is rare for an individual to specify his or her goals in life before settling down to work toward them.

We seem to vacillate between pressures (to find a job or a place to live), impulses (to get married, to have children), and external programming (to consume). These three sources of motivation express themselves enough to give us a reassuring sense of constantly having plans.

But are these plans authentically our own? Have we chosen them? Do we think about them regularly? Asking the question point-blank is apt to provoke evasive answers.

Now, we cannot achieve mastery of time for our own benefit without clear goals and without the permanent application of our will power. Our mastery will reduce to tricks of time management, like making more economical use of the telephone and avoiding overlong meetings.

It is advisable to structure our time around our goals because the art of time, like that of governing, consists in making choices—we face more possibilities than hours in which to realize them.

One British humorist said that the only important question in life is: "What do I do next?" This must be a preliminary step in the organization of our time, for the question does indeed arise several times a day: we are creatures of action who, as Pascal once noted, find it almost impossible to sit for an hour doing nothing. To answer the question without going too far wrong, we obviously must refer to something broader: our plans, expressed in goals that are ordered by priorities.

But our goals have an even larger role than dividing up each year or half hour into various activities. Goals give our time meaning and allow us to measure results.

To make us flourish, our actions must have a meaning and involve progress.

To give an action meaning, we must be able to connect it with something outside it: a goal. Determining progress requires giving the goal specific content.

When the three conditions of choice, meaning, and progress are met, we have a much easier time answering Titus's evening question about whether we've made good use of our time today. And more often with a *yes*.

Thus, goals are technically indispensable, for they constitute the grid of choices implied by the optimal use of our time. They also are psychologically indispensable for establishing the bases of our satisfaction.

How do we go about setting our goals? Probably by a certain affirmation of the self. For a person cannot know what he or she wants without already having a good idea who he or she is.

Teenagers who are asked, "What would you like to do later on?" too often reply, "I don't know," because in many cases they are going through a period of life where their identity is still unfocused.

After all, a strengthening of the self is also desirable to ensure that our goals are indeed ours and not those of others. Between the goals we have gotten directly from our parents, those of the organization we belong to, and those resulting from the emotional pressures inflicted by those around us, what place is left for our legitimate demands?

Legitimate? Not everyone believes in a self-evident right to his or her own goals. The Judeo-Christian culture we've been raised in subtly preaches self-effacement. And adopting the goals that others project on us relieves us of the need to ask too-searching questions about ourselves.

Now, the time for living better is definitely our own. If we are not completely involved with it, who then will be so for us? The progress we want to make presupposes a minimum of rational egoism. Some people have nothing to prove in this area; others should do a bit of gentle violence to themselves and begin looking after number one.

The allocation of time that is truly our own will require something more than just this new frame of mind. We will have to take a detailed look at our schedules, and our mode of functioning, to distinguish between the activities we have chosen freely and the ones that are merely responses to the routines and urgings of the people around us.

A few days spent noting down where each hour of our professional and personal time goes, and considering how they add up, will result in an inexpensive and often instructive check-up.

Make a detailed examination of how you use your time, and for each action systematically ask yourself: "Did I really want to?"

Next, a tad better informed about what is actually going on, and resolved to throw a few pinches of "me first" into the system, we will earnestly ask ourselves where to begin determining our plans.

We should first recoginize a basic goal that in principle we share with all our peers, even though it is rarely made explicit. Two thousand five hundred years ago, Buddha formulated it negatively when he declared that man's first duty was to avoid suffering.

Twenty-five centuries later, the French biologist Henri Laborit, citing his experiments and analysis of the structure of the brain, declared: "Everything we do is in the pursuit of pleasure"—hence, the avoidance of displeasure.

In the collective unconscious the word *pleasure* still has a bad reputation. What would we think of someone who declared: "My one lone aim in life is to maximize my pleasure"? An egoist, an affected hedonist? Nevertheless, the only difference between him and us, insists

Laborit, is that he says so and we do so without proclaiming it or, rather, without realizing it.

But, actually, I spend a good part of my time doing things I'd rather not do.

Of course. But those are the things that make it possible for you to get what will give you pleasure, and also keep you out of much greater displeasure, like being without a job.

Perhaps. But I perform some actions purely out of duty, because I am bound for reasons of friendship or family. They bring me nothing but bother.

I'm not sure. Don't they enhance your merit in your own eyes and in those of others? That's an essential pleasure.

What about the masochists who do themselves harm?

Precisely the point. They love it.

And suicide? Surely that's not done for pleasure.

In a way it is. When a person kills himself, it's to put an end to an anguish that's judged (wrongly or rightly) worse than death.

To introduce this principle of pleasure or non-suffering at the start of a few thoughts about the goals of life is to urge a cleansing lucidity about oneself. What if there were no true altruists, but only egoists whose personal programming leads them to find pleasure in pleasing others?

And what if our "duties" were either tests we need in order to feel that we were good people, or needless constraints that we did not have the nerve to shrug off? The message of Buddha, joined by Laborit and many others, is that of a joyous modesty.

Let us not make ourselves more deserving than we are, and admit our desire to succeed in life, for certainly no one will take over the job for us.

In this spirit of critical lucidity, let us take on the time for planning, the time for exploring our goals. Like any piece of research, it is good idea to conduct it in two stages: an opening and a closing.

First, the opening—where we are free to entertain any idea that comes to mind, no matter how high or low the plan's probability or feasibility is. In the first step we make a close study of ourselves, entering with curiosity into the world of our wishes, desires, ambitions, and fantasies.

Later, in the closing stage, passing our harvest through the sieves of realism and method, we will set the goals that will give meaning to the effort to master our time.

During the opening stage, we may conduct our research into our usual areas, professional or personal.

But we should not forget time, of course, since it is at present the center of the concerns. If after reading these pages it seems logical to determine your goals, those that will result in your using your time better should be given priority.

By reading the previous chapters you probably encountered the description of familiar problems or the mention of tempting solutions. You are thus in a position to make a more precise and complete diagnosis of your difficulties with time. (If you haven't noted any, you can easily go through the preceding pages in this chapter and identify your commonest obstacles or weaknesses. Underline the ones that seem the most urgent, and you will know [by which door] to start rearranging your time).

In doing this, you first will see projects or problems connected with your activity at work. This is one of the more familiar parts of the investigation, and of the two areas explored, it is the one about which each of us is assumed to devote the most thought.

It is practical to classify plans and problems into categories. Thus, we may want to obtain a profit-sharing scheme, launch a new product, and go on a study trip of the Middle East. We may even want to do all these things at the same time. These are not a priori incompatible but reveal different aspects of ourselves, our thinking, and our work rhythms.

A classification like this that allows for a better definition of our joys and times of action sets the scene for the ultimate stage of choice.

Thus you review the goals you share with your organization. These are often quantifiable (volume, gross receipts, profit margin) and usually dated (monthly program, annual or medium-term plan).

Next, take a look at the goals concerning the people working under you. These goals may involve the material organization, personal relations, work assignments, the system of communication.

Finally, think of yourself, the daily actor in this world of work: pursuing a career, seeking high pay, not disdaining certain roles or titles, giving and following instructions, alternately needing security and change, hoping to increase your creativity, training, and experience.

There is material here for many projections into the future, with the aim of seeing how these situations could be improved; hence a new list of themes develops in an area we know a good deal about. Let us try to distinguish their orders of urgency and importance.

Next comes the second area, that of life in general where our work takes up the lion's share of the time, but also allows an essential part of ourselves to bloom.

There are still many other areas in which we seek personal realization. For each point mentioned, we may ask ourselves four questions: *Does this concern me? Where am I with respect to it today? Where do I want to go from here? In what length of time?*

We all may wish to have in our lives specific times available in the following areas (listed in no particular order):

1. Time for the body. Maintenance, exercise, grooming, realizing that it may give us real satisfaction if we take a bit of care of it.

2. Leisure time. Movies, television, concerts, or theater: when are we available? dinners, parties, various events: will we find pleasure in them? Games, sports (viewing or playing): do we know how to have fun?

3. Time for sensuality. Does pleasure have the place

and time in our life that it deserves? Do we remain within our fantasies? Are we at ease with the animal that we are?

4. Time for consumption. Running errands without stress and without haste; then being able to arrange, handle, store—in short, benefiting from the objects we've brought into our lives.

5. Time for travel. Discovery, adventure, or simply a change of scene and vacations. Being somewhere else transforms and refreshes us, but takes a lot of time; do we have enough of it?

6. Time for rest. Do we get the right amount of sleep, recovery time, unconstricted weekends? Or are we dipping into the capital of our health?

7. Time for love. A successful relationship is totally absorbing. No one has yet managed to put tenderness in pill form or intimacy on index cards. Time appears to be to love what the sun is to plant life. Are we getting enough exposure?

8. Time for others. Friendship is not holding up well these days. With all we have to do, something has to go. Are you resigned to this? "Others" may also be your community to which you would like to participate more fully, or some other generous plan. When?

9. Time for family. Ceremonies, outings, or collective hugs. Our parents as well as our children would very much like a bit of our time, and they express this with reproach or discretion. And don't we also need them?

10. Time for reading. Newspapers just glanced at and books barely started make us ashamed and wishful.

Going past a book store, we turn our eyes away so as not to increase our regret. Are we resigned to living ignorantly?

11. Time for development. Young people come on the scene speaking foreign languages and tapping away at computers, but even an adult has a right to go on learning. We know, don't we, that we are still capable of it. But it takes a lot of time.

12. Time for creating. Our professional work is too often predictable and repetitive. Rare is the job that encourages self-expression. Every one of us would like to find out if he or she is a musician, author, painter, or inventor.

13. Time for meditating. Beauty, the Milky Way, nature or Zen beckon us. Life speeds by like a turbotrain and we still don't know what we are doing here. Metaphysical or poetic questions are currently on the increase. If we dared, we would explore them.

14. Time for regression. When was the last time we rolled around on the grass like children or animals? Do we still know how to play the buffoon or sing at the top of our lungs? Inside all of us there's a kid who will play tricks on us if he is never allowed to show his face.

15. Time for solitude. Except during some work-connected travel, in the inspiring setting of a Holiday Inn or Howard Johnson, when do we enjoy a bit of solitude? How can we know what we have to say to ourselves if we never meet ourself face to face? Few of us want to live completely alone, but who wouldn't like a little solitude now and then?

These fifteen varied kinds of time may not exhaust all our potentialities or desires, but it is certain that this subjective and schematic list suggests paths rarely taken, secret guilts, worlds admittedly unexplored.

Can a whole person live fifteen lives at a time in the attempt not to miss something essential? Necessity forces us to make choices and thus to sacrifice something—after mature reflection, if possible.

This work on our goals touches something deep in us and so may spark resistance. For who among us can claim to maintain an absolutely clear understanding of himself or herself?

If we already feel frustrated by our inability to accomplish what we wish, isn't it an indignity to add on other unsatisfied desires that we blessedly weren't thinking of?

We already know that life is too short and the conditions of our existence too pinched. So why add to the list of things inaccessible and aggravate the torment of Tantalus? (What we don't think about won't bother us.)

This objection is understandable but implies that the present constraints cannot be appreciably eased: "I'm reading a book on the art of managing one's time, but it won't work for me. So . . ."

We tend to believe our doctor when he or she says: "You're short of breath. Your lungs don't get enough air. If you do these exercises every day for three months, your lung capacity will increase by 30 percent, and you'll be able to run without becoming exhausted." We admit that we can change our body, and this is just as true of our habits and attitudes. Perhaps even more true, but the media have not yet hammered away at this truth the way they have about the virtues of aerobic exercise.

So the inquiry into one's goals is doubly worth the trouble if you want to loosen the iron collar of time. Because you'll be able to accomplish more and because this is the time to realize that. For it may be that among the things you hadn't yet thought of, you will discover more important and satisfying projects than the ones you currently have.

Another common objection: we may have obsessive desires, typically centering on our sexuality, that are thought to be inadmissible. All the same, we cannot equate them with the desire to double sales in the next two years or to reread Shakespeare.

Why not? It is characteristic of the inadmissible that we think of it very often, reflect about it rarely, and almost never talk about it (except to our therapist). But a clear-sighted exploration of ourselves cannot be limited to what's on public display.

Faced with an inadmissible desire, we may imagine four thoughtful positions:

1. Deciding to satisfy it and take the necessary steps;
2. Summoning the inner strength required to sublimate it (cheers!);
3. Talking about it with some qualified person so as to give yourself a mental airing and, all things considered, remaining unsatisfied. But at least things will have been considered and a line drawn between enduring and taking charge.

I think I already hear the objection: "What is this gimcrack psychologizing? Things are never that simple. We aren't computers." I'm aware of that, thank-you very much.

In response, allow me to spell out three of my biases (I have many others):

1. I have the impression that we are living in an era where we attack problems by spraying clouds of words at them rather than trying with modesty and inevitable groping to solve them (deliciously summarized by Marshall McLuhan: "When everything will have been said and done, more will have been said than done.")

2. In cases of doubt or anxiety, the use of reflection always seems to me more fruitful than its absence.

3. This absence of reflection shows up most clearly in ourselves.

Isn't it time for a change?

Let's close this parenthesis and get back to our goals.

The principle of favoring reflection leads me to deal with the last common objection: "We cannot plan ourselves like a business enterprise. In my private life, I need improvisation, intuition, impulsivity."

How true that is! And how I regret (nearly every day) that we do not live in a bucolic society where our spontaneity would flower so much more!

But it is just because we don't apply the same systematic spirit to the pursuit of our private goals that our professional goals take up the lion's share of our time and we save for our other goals mere scraps of time.

Existential crises occur when what we truly want has no place in the life we lead. Why not give our dreams the help of a bit of method?

Here is a bit. You have already visited three areas: your time, your profession, your life—an arbitrary partitioning, for all three go together, but a practical one.

For each of your three lists, you can underline the three or four most important goals. A dozen goals will stand out from the rest.

To ensure that they are the good ones (on the first try, we always forget important ones) and that they are indeed your own, try two new gambits:

For each goal, ask yourself whether it comes from inside or outside. In other words, is it a demand or constraint issuing from the people around you (some are excellent, like "Stop smoking!") or a personal desire expressive of your freedom and independence? Then consider the proportion obtained.

There is no score or prize to win. To each the dish of his or her choice. The important thing is to become aware of it.

Another approach: take a blank page and do the "last six months of your life" test. Imagine that your life will suddenly end in six months, while you are in good health and full possession of your faculties. What would you like to be sure of experiencing during this final half year? Now you may think of projects that hadn't figured on your lists and that would be appropriate to add to them.

Next, take the time necessary (it may be a few days) to let all these goals settle, be thought through and reclassified. You will then have a dozen essential goals in various areas and also a well-stocked reserve of other important goals. You will already have learned something new about yourself. And you will be wondering where to begin.

Consider, for the sake of simplicity, that you have found two kinds of goals: "operational goals" and "life goals." Each of us will draw the line between them where it suits us. The two categories have different functions and lend themselves to different treatments.

Let's begin with the operational goals. They are more short-term—one day to one year—and concern more or less immediate actions. Here we find, "Take my son to a football game," "Buy a home computer," and "Find a replacement for my assistant." You can recognize them from the fact that they must in principle be

• Measurable or able to be assigned a date for beginning a plan of action;
• Precise and concrete (avoid "Not being late"; instead write "Arriving three minutes early at the meeting Monday morning");
• Realistic;
• Satisfying (be sure you find them truly to your taste);
• Fractionable (avoid discouragement by trying to take on too much right away).

Life goals natually stretch over long periods of time

(like learning Spanish, becoming your own boss, developing your powers of concentration, or even retiring at fifty-five to a farmhouse in Provence). There's no need for them to be realistic; perhaps even, as we shall see, the opposite is the case. Here, the desire's intensity counts more than its probability of realization.

But such as they are, these goals perform several valuable functions. First, they help us broaden our temporal horizon by getting us to think five to twenty years into the future.

Once gained, this horizon will not be too hard to preserve or reconstruct. We will need it often.

Logically, it enhances our ability to find meaning in our life—a cornerstone that one soon loses in the press of modern life. For want of perceiving its metaphysical "meaning," a clearer view of what we want to accomplish or know gives our days and months greater meaning.

It should be noted in this regard that life goals may undergo important changes, if not each week, then at least once or twice a year. So we cannot consider them fixed for all time. Looking at them every six months with a fresh eye helps us measure both what has changed in our lives and our own growth.

The most important use of life goals, however, probably is to enable us to get beyond ourselves and unflinchingly to brave the rigors of our existence.

A study done fifteen years ago by the psychologist Charles A. Garfield clearly shows this capacity. He set about determining how "high-performance" individuals differed from other people.

His subjects were persons who unquestionably performed better in sports, education, business, medicine, and the arts and who went further in their careers than other people. These persons were not supermen, but did share a particular approach to their problems, goals, and risks.

Soviet researchers are also doing similar research, calling this new discipline "anthropomaximology."

After examining the behavior of some 1,200 of his "achievers," Garfield found four shared characteristics:

1. What they do, they accomplish "for the art," as a function of demanding internal goals;

2. They solve problems instead of asking who is to blame.

3. They take their risks confidently, once they have considered what may happen if all goes wrong.

4. They mentally rehearse the actions and events ahead.

Furthermore, they know when to stop, take vacations, avoid stress, and not let themselves be swamped by detail and have mastered the art of delegating work.

But the most interesting finding was their ability to make the best of their goals. We have seen, in fact, that we possessed three trump cards concerning goals: predicting, wanting, and preparing. Of the three it is the last, preparing, that is least utilized.

Everyone knows, in fact, how to anticipate an important appointment at 3:00 P.M. Many people—not all—arrive at the appointment with some idea of what they want. But few have imagined various scenarios for the interview and have prepared themselves for any eventuality. We don't have a clear idea of how much room there is to maneuver with the person we are meeting with, who may have done this preparation. Now, this is not a gift but a mental technique we can practice. For example, we may list the possible obstacles to each goal.

The worst-case scenario reduces anxiety. Before they set out on a project, Garfield's high performers hypothesized about its failure and decided whether they would be able to live with failure. If they decided they could, they were relieved of anxiety about failure and sailed boldly into action.

So we realize that it is not enough to formulate our goals. We then must learn to keep them actively in mind, revising them and examining them from every angle to anticipate both satisfactions and problems. By "inhabiting" them in advance, our chances of success and of benefiting from them show notable improvement.

This technique of mentally rehearsing the future is used by people who want to surpass themselves. Recall the Olympic slalomers. Thomas Tutko of the California State University at San Jose trains champion skiers to vividly imagine themselves beating their own records and feeling what would then be going on within themselves. They may then more easily perform the feat that they had imaginatively experienced.

This technique works, and happily, it works just as well in everyday life: our own. Why and how it works is not yet clear. But the oldest schools of wisdom know that our unconscious harbors an energy that few of us bother to turn to account.

Now, methods of self-programming yield valuable results. For them, there's no need to worry about the realistic nature of the goal, nor about the necessary means. These methods are centered on the most concrete possible definition of the goal and on the visualization of its outcome. Next, we set about making ourselves receptive to soak up, through concentration, the firm conviction that our goal will be achieved.

The chances of success are not 100 percent, but they are sufficiently improved for us to imagine that our unconscious has given us a helping hand.

The time for planning is one for the intensive use of our powers of prediction, volition, and preparation. We contain untapped reserves that will provide the fuel needed for the work we must accomplish each day to master our time.

MY FRIEND TIME

❖

Time or life • Doing everything at the same time
Treating it like a friend • Forgetting nothing
My datebook next to my heart • My second memory
How to be dependable • Down with stress
Appointment with time • Dashboard for the day
The ecology of time • Personal appraisal.

We all know the power of words. They lead us closer to knowledge, launch us into the imaginary, and color reality to our taste. They can also cause us to take black for white. For the images or ideas evoked by overused words prevent us from thinking more deeply or broadly.

For instance, take a few common phrases with the word *time* and replace it with *life*. So rather than "That takes time," we have "That takes life." Make this substitution in each of the following, and notice what happens in your mind:

- No *time* for
- I don't have the *time*
- Using my *time* well
- Losing *time*
- I'm going to spend some *time* on it
- I need more *time*
- Mastering my *time*

Need I say more? Using *life* rather than *time* shows that for the individual they are in practice one and the same thing.

This is what gives our quest for the mastery of time all the importance it must assume—namely, vital.

This book has dealt mainly with ideas and principles, a common mode of communication in our culture. Between brains that have been similarly programmed, there is mutual understanding and . . . that saves time.

But the risk is to remain abstract, theoretical, at a distance, although we are dealing with something that concerns and affects us: our lives. So we must be able to apply all these ideas to life as it it is actually lived— which is a problem for me, for I am truly knowledgeable about only one life, my own.

So without either pretension or false modesty, I will try in this concluding chapter to situate these ideas and principles in a life I can speak about with some authority. For it is not as a philosopher or organizational specialist that I am competent to sermonize about time. More simply, I found myself, like you, confronted with but unprepared for a problem with my time. I immediately realized that this question involved essentials and so had to be grappled with.

Since I was self-educated in matters of time, it took me years to make any progress, trying out systems or attitudes, honing my tools and then more years to coordinate them and achieve some coherence. Meanwhile, I compared my concerns and solutions with those of my friends or acquaintances who were similarly pressed for time. Every day, I never stopped thinking about time.

Looking from the outside, some people might believe that I became a perfectionist about time. But would we say that someone was a perfectionist about life? If so, I would readily concede the justice of this criticism, for in my personal system (to each his own) life is the supreme value—not faith, not my country, not equality, not order, and not even justice—life, respect for it, the religion of it, and the love of it, and thus, not far behind, freedom.

Pardon the credo, which in our day smacks of pedantic vanity. But just as we need goals, I believe that we need a system of clear values to assist us in the quest for a mastery over an element as all-encompassing as time. Any thing that disturbs, spoils, drains, reduces, and shortens life is abhorrent to me, and I make every effort to avoid or at least to reduce it. And I notice that I can often do this by directly or indirectly acting with and on time.

When we put life at the very center of our thoughts, we derive from it first self-respect, then respect for others (who are extensions of ourselves, our nourishing milieu), and finally graciousness, the need for a personal ecology and a rejection of stress.

Self-respect is governed by a desire for balance among the main point of interest in our lives: work, family, creativity, sensory pleasures, culture, travel, and so forth.

In our day, if we want to be among the best in some area, the lack of time obliges us to accept our being among less than average in many other areas.

This is the syndrome of the "grind," of his favorite sport, his career, his hobby, his children. I've seen artists increasingly cut themselves off from everything outside their creation. I've spent time with politicians who "made a gift" of their persons to their electors. I've known many executives who corroborate the American wisecrack: "When you've had enough of seeing a man, marry him!" But I have also seen many men and women who value their family life so much that they put themselves out of the running in every other area.

Every achievement is paid for by sacrifices. This is an essential choice that must be respected. But life seems to me much too various, too attractive to be amputated. The only achievement I aspired to was to have every iron in the fire, to leave not the smallest stone unturned as a possible source of life. And each stone required that time be devoted to it.

This was when for each activity, proposal, encounter, or act of consumption, I got into the habit of determining the time to reserve for it so that it would not get lost in the shuffle.

In order to keep variety in my life, I paradoxically had to learn to do a good deal of refusing, and so to estimate beforehand the life interest of everything that came up, from a dinner invitation (was it worth the hours of sleep it would cost?) to the launching of a new business venture (who will have to handle it? me? at the expense of whom or what?).

To choose our time better, we must know ourselves better or become better informed about what life offers us.

With the same concern for balance, I wanted no more than a year to go by without my doing something significant. I feared I might lose my taste for living in the rat race in which we find ourselves stuck if we are not careful.

Hence the need for plans and goals. In order to create, learn, or build anything, I realized that it had to be desired, willed, and then anticipated. I could mobilize my limited supply of time/energy without forgoing everything else only if I programmed it far enough in advance. Deciding to devote four weeks to writing when that is not your chief occupation seemed to smack of dreaming—unless one began getting organized for this purpose six to twelve months ahead of time.

Obviously, I lost some spontaneity and easygoingness. I discussed the matter with people in businesses where you can never predict what's going to happen or who prefer deciding where to go for their vacation at the last minute and who always will find a room. I observed that they sometimes managed to have wonderful journeys and sometimes disastrous ones. My own preference was for more regularity, at the cost of a small investment of time. Made on time.

A Spaniard said that time was a gentlemen. Rather than do battle with it, I learned to get it on my side and to win its support.

Becoming a friend of time means treating it like a friend by devoting some time to it.

The better I could estimate the time something was going to take, the proper moment for fitting it in, possible conflicts, the more things went the way I expected and without too many hitches.

When my project was completed, I felt a certain joy at having painstakingly shaped the most precious of raw materials: time.

Like all of us, I need others for my happiness and personal development. But staying as alive as possible seems to require making continual gains in autonomy, the only way to enable me to be unafraid of change. Another aspect of self-respect is not depending on others, which means, among other things, forgetting nothing.

To let others decide my time would be to delegate my life to them. Certainly, none of us is completely free here. Because we work, we devote a daily bloc of some eight to eleven hours to the organization we work for. How we use a large part of these hours is beyond our control. If we work on an assembly line we cannot claim any of that time; if we are in management or the professions we can control less than half of our time.

Even if half my work time is lost to me, that amounts to little more than five hours a day. There still remain at least nineteen hours over which I have some say. But I have observed how much people whose business it is to make decisions will, paradoxically, tend to leave the organization of their hours to routine, their secretaries, or their spouses. Perhaps they see some value, if their lives don't suit them, in being able to blame someone else?

I instinctively consider any surrender of the power of decision about my only irreplaceable capital—my time—as an abdication. In the Old West, cowboys alluded to their independence by fondling the butt of the revolver at their hip. I myself carry my datebook next to my heart, and when I take off my jacket, I always place it within reach.

In this small, essential notebook are recorded all the transactions in the stock market of my hours. Who else could trade them with full knowledge? Who else wants to know whether somebody I must meet will be concise or long-winded; whether I need to stop at home before getting my train; whether the importance of a certain meeting requires an hour's prior preparation; whether after this appointment, I should telephone to confirm certain points?

Rather than manage our time table we should chisel it out. It is wiser to hand over our checkbook to someone else than to hand over our datebook.

At a time when I docilely responded to the demands of my friends and colleagues and readily gave away the hourly slices of my day, a commercial was shown during the intermission in French movie theaters. A little bear had his basket of eskimo pies picked clean by a forest of hands. He clutched the last one, wailing: "No, not mine!"

I soon had the same sense of anxious possessiveness about "my" hours. The common error of penciling in only our appointments with others gives them a de facto priority in the allotment of our time. If we are not continually alert to this fact, we will soon find we are running short of time for ourselves.

The critical hours, the ones that make a difference, are precisely those where we can be alone to reflect, to study, to anticipate, and even to create. It is these most important times that we often fail to set aside on our calendars. One further step toward autonomy: I have regularly made appointments with myself at least once a week.

But if we aspire to autonomy and the control of our future, it is not enough to keep a calendar. We need to do more in order not to forget anything. In an expanding world, with fragmented activities, forgetting is a venial but enduring sin. We forget our own ideas, then tasks to do, and then commitments made. We could even make this into a general rule: the amount level of forgetting increases as a square of overactivity.

What we forget always gets its revenge, catching up with us at the very worst moment in the form of a loss of time, money, or energy—or all three at once.

The mastery of our time begins with the mastery of our memory.

Because my own memory is less than foolproof, this limitation has led to a change my behavior. I had to find a more trustworthy system. I happen to have inherited three things from my father: a pair of gold cuff links, a love of dogs, and a habit of writing on small memo pads. I now know that these little rectangles of white paper are much more precious than banknotes, and I owe a large part of my effectiveness to them.

For each passing idea, a memo; for each thing to do, a memo. And only one item per memo, which is thrown away when the idea has served its purpose or the thing has been done. What makes this system terrific is that one can put a pad in every room of one's home (and in one's pocket) and one can easily project each memo into the future. So there is no excuse for not immediately writing down what crosses your mind and, even if it concerns something six weeks away, for not remembering it when the day comes.

An example: in six weeks I'm going to London, and today I think I'll need to take with me a copy of a contract. I take a memo and write down the date of the eve of my departure. That day, it will show up when I am getting my papers together for the trip.

How will it show up? Thanks to a standard size folder with thirty-two compartments (one for each day of the month, plus one for what goes beyond a month), which I call my cardboard Memory and which relieves my own memory of all these details and frees it up for what is important, creative, or fun.

Something as simple as the daily use of mini memos (I happen to write out thirty to forty a day) achieves a sureness of operation that strengthens one's self-confidence. And also the confidence that others have in you.

Concerning others, one element I consider essential lies in what I call availability/reliability. It seems to me that the individual becomes truly adult and mature only when others may begin counting on him or her. Who? Those close to him, bosses, coworkers, customers, parents and friends (even those vaguely defined as such).

Count on what? The minimum would be a little attention and the following through on this attention. The little society we are evolving in is full of supervisors whose subordinates cannot manage to collar them for a talk or a signature. And with those people who do not return calls, rarely answer letters, or follow up agreements only long afterward, if ever.

Feeling myself (unfortunately?) bound by every promise, no matter how trivial, I had to go about keeping those promises. In other words, not to find myself short of the time it would take, and to set out the necessary reminders so I won't forget. Here, memos are of invaluable assistance to me.

Although many people are lacking in courtesy, it is not just because they are ill bred. They make appointments indiscriminately and find they are swamped; they accept too many contacts and obligations and cannot live up to them.

Contrary to what most people think, it is much easier to say no than to say yes. A yes is already a commitment, an option on the future, an obligation to follow through. It is better to be parsimonious with one's yeses.

Saying no may be an unpleasant moment, but it passes quickly—especially when we have the grace to use a little tact with it. The person making the request may be slightly disappointed, but understands. We want to say yes in order to please and to get approval, but won't the other person be entitled to resent more a yes that is not followed through than an affable but immediate no? I much prefer to treat a few people well than to disappoint great numbers of them.

At work and even within the family, harmonious relationships require a good comprehension of the time of others as well as one's own. This is obvious when we ask for a coworker's assistance or for the boss's ear. We need to know enough about their present situation to have some idea whether they have time to comply with our request. That way we manage to avoid being a pest.

This is also advisable with the people working under us. A wrong note is hit when poor preparation on my part makes me late and forces someone under me to work overtime or at all hours.

Genuine emergencies are rare. Errors of anticipation are legion.

The modern basis of respect for the other person comes down to deeming his or her time at least as valuable as one's own and acting accordingly.

Thus, one of the least-respected (small) commitments concerns the length of discussions. Because we dare not ask for a whole hour, we say, "It'll take twenty minutes," but we are still at it after forty-five. This is not very serious, even if we then tell ourselves that the other person should have guessed and expected more.

Some exceptions can be announced in advance, but most work discussions should last no more than an hour. And since there often is a lot that must be gone over, it is not enough just to avoid chit-chat. Prior preparation is imperative. That is why I drew up a sheet of "guide for discussions" that impels me to reflect a little more than would a simple order of the day. When I expect that the number and importance of the topics will take up more than an hour, I can either postpone discussion of some of them for another time or warn my interlocutor.

In the latter case, I give him or her a copy. We have our plan of work and can decide together to speed up the discussion in order to cover everything.

Finally, when those close to us have an important problem, nothing is more frustrating than to be unable to give them right away all the time that they need or that will relieve them. Managing to do this without neglecting all our other duties means we do not regard this kind of interruption as aberrant, but that we have uses of time that are not stretched as tightly as the strings on a guitar.

For a long time I admired men in a hurry. Until I realized that they were merely under stress.

What I fear most about stress is not that it kills, but that it prevents one from savoring life.

I know it because as a young executive I lived this way for a number of years. It took me years to notice that I was missing out on important things (reflection, beauty, the sun, the taste of things, my children's childhoods) and also that one didn't need to be overstressed to be productive.

Individuals who are prone to stress are often what psychologists call Type A personalities. We recognize them by their tendencies to try to do too many things in too little time and to become tense and irritated with themselves and others.

Now, Type A persons are not necessarily more effective than others. While taking a mathematics test, Type As secreted four time as much adrenalin as Type Bs, and their blood pressure increased at triple the rate of Type Bs—as though these simple acts seemed threatening.

Since I was of an entrepreneurial temperament, I long wondered whether I was a Type A personality. For reassurance, I looked for practical solutions.

My trying to do too many things in too little time seemed to result from a mixture of inexperience and lack of organization. My inexperience, which fortunately evaporated with the years, prevented me from appreciating how long it took to carry out a particular act. So I took time to observe and to measure, until I had a sense of how long I spent on tasks.

My lack of organization spawned the classic errors: disorder on my desk (the mere sight of it drained my energy), an absence of definite priorities; resultant difficulties in estimating how much progress I'd made in a day; a tendency to do several things at the same time or do the same thing several times; a vague sense of following a zigzag course.

I realized I had to stop reacting by trying to go even faster. On the contrary, I cultivated the reflex "Stop, and drop everything" every time the motor began racing. And, little by little, I managed to slow down without impairing the quality of my output.

It was at this point that I introduced what I now feel is the key to organization: the daily "appointment with time" in which I fix my "plan for the day" and that enables me not to lose the thread of it. I began to glimpse "the" secret.

Just as we help put out a forest fire by lighting a counterfire, we should fight the lack of time by devoting time to thinking about the use of our time: to give time to time.

Have we not heard that the success of the Apollo moon landing was due less to technology than to tremendous preparation? Aren't we beginning to realize that it is the amount of time the Japanese spend studying their decisions that makes their implementation so remarkable? Why didn't I realize sooner that my day, too, was a landing on the moon? Less complicated and perilous, but more frequent! What ensured the success of one would be likely to enhance the other—the time for reflection and preparation.

So I made an "appointment with time" each morning before breakfast, a moment when no one can distract me. Then, in the calm of the early morning, according to a ritual and with the proper tools, I live my day for the first time— mentally.

Since we are self-programmed, we should take particular care that no one else does it for us. The sheet with the plan for the day that I fill out during this preparation includes everything that is currently foreseeable.

I then keep the day's plan constantly in front of me, like a dashboard. What has been concluded may be crossed out, what unexpectedly crops up is written down right away, so as to visualize the conflicts of time. And it is natural that there regularly are some.

It is impossible to eliminate all disruptions, but it is essential to pinpoint them promptly in relation to one's schedule.

Taking a detached look at what is going on is soothing to the nerves, for it dispels any sense of confusion.

By the evening, it is rare that I have achieved everything I had planned. That isn't serious if during the day I could choose what could unproblematically be deferred.

Mastering one's time is not a daily ordeal in a limited amount of time. I think of it as controlling the flow of water every day to irrigate a spot in the garden that needs it most—neither too much nor too little.

I realized my system was beginning to work when, in the evening, instead of stress, I felt the satisfaction of not having at any point let go of the steering wheel.

From then on, I could seek a better ecology of my time, trying to find more natural rhythms—for example, in cleansing my time of the often irritating dust of our minor obligations.

No more than anyone else do I dote on paperwork or attending all the minutiae involved in doing a thorough job. We cannot get away from these things, but I have concentrated them between my "appointment with time" and a quick work session with my secretary at the start of the day. All incoming mail, documents to be signed, notes, or nonurgent calls coming in the rest of the day are put on hold until the next morning.

Just as mini memos or index cards enable us to free our minds, my planning at the start of the day frees the subsequent hours from the commonest or most avoidable interruptions.

I later learned that this was the method of the great economist John Maynard Keynes. In two hours of concentrated effort in the morning, he made all his important decisions and then didn't think about work for the rest of the day. He went to galleries and attended ballets.

Then I let my secretary do the work I have given her. If I was frequently interrupting her to take some dictation or to get so-and-so on the telephone, she would lose the autonomy of her time, hence her efficiency.

I realized that time was neutral and that it was up to me to give it importance and color. Thus, one way to reduce the time devoted to minutiae was to sharpen my judgment about what was truly important and productive.

My goals gave relief and perspective. The longer aim I take, the less time I am forced to spend on things that do not serve any really significant purpose. In managing my time, I manage myself like some costly machine.

I have sometimes wondered what goes through the minds of those great consultants or lawyers who charge hundreds of dollars an hour for their services. Do they still have it in them to load up a cart in a supermarket, to go to the movies, to have a drink with a friend? It must be disquieting to be able to put a price on one's minutes. But it is no less important than knowing the value of it.

We can get even more mileage out of the master idea of devoting time to time. Although less indispensable than the morning's appointment with time, setting up a similar one for the evening adds a new dimension to life. For if we do not do enough prior preparation, still less do we examine after the fact. Nevertheless, this is a simple means of personal inquiry. To recall at the end of the day what has happened, and why it happened this way, for good or ill: there are obvious lessons to be learned from this examination of our own attitude and reactions that it would be a pity to deprive ourselves of.

Here again, there's nothing very new under the sun. Five centuries before Christ, the Stoics practiced this retrospection, and during the Second World War every bombing mission was preceded by a briefing and followed by a debriefing.

Comparing what really happened with what was expected is worth more than a hundred pages of theory about our way of treating time.

The counterfire principle also has an interesting application in combating my periodic urges to procrastinate. I believe I am not the only person who, when faced with a certain chore, finds it hard to get down to work. Anything will serve as a pretext not to begin: getting a cup of coffee, reading a newspaper article, making a telephone call—in short, delaying the plunge. To fight this force of inertia, one Zen Buddhist method consists of using precisely inertia.

Do nothing. Truly nothing. Remain seated with one's hands on one's knees, eye closed, attempting to produce a void in one's mind. Dismiss every thought, every image, except perhaps that of still waters, and let waves of calm roll over yourself by breathing deeply.

Keep this up until you feel in a state of true inertia, mental and physical. Then slowly reopen your eyes . . . and immediately take up the task at which you were balking.

There are many other recipes, a host of tricks for managing our time. We can introduce simplifications and improvements every time we think about a commonplace situation (how we deal with the telephone, meetings, travel, secretarial help, filing, delegation of work, and so on). Scores of "how to" books on this topic have been published that promote the rationalizing of office life. Valuably complementing my own practices, they have been a source of inspiration to me in my own operations.

One day, I recognized that with my problems with time I was just one case among many, so numerous were the people who went on leading unsatisfactory lives because they had not had occasion to focus on solutions.

Apparently ever more numerous. I had been impressed this way by a survey that showed that in the five years between 1978 and 1982 the proportion of Frenchworkers whose working hours conflicted with their family or personal life went from 28 to 43.5 percent!

I must conclude with a candid balance sheet of how the application of these principles and the use of these tools has changed my life:

1. *I work no less:* Without totally imitating my friend and colleague Jean Boissonnat, editor-in-chief of the publications I oversee, (who says: "I find that working thirty-five hours a week is such a great idea that I do it twice a week"), I start work early and knock off late. But I can say that it is by conscious choice, for I love what I do and it is one of my ways of having fun. While I could have more leisure time, I deliberately have not done so.

2. *I concentrate on essentials.* And this, to me, is the big difference. Always thinking of the best possible use of my time, I never waste it. I always find time to do what's important. The proof: I have managed to write this book (about two hundred fifty hours' work) without sacrificing anything important among my various responsibilities.

3. *I am not overstressed.* I took a test on predispositions to stress, where vulnerability to stress began at thirty points and became serious at fifty. I scored a six, which fully confirmed that one can be productive without falling into the Type A category.

4. *I capitalize on life:* even though I don't have a great deal of "free time," I savor each hour of my private life. I have learned to look forward to it with pleasure (even before breakfast) and to live every hour with my mind free of the "problems" that I know to deal with during the hours set aside for them.

5. *I need to make progress:* I am not a master of time, merely an apprentice. Now that I have sampled the rewards of more malleable time, I measure the whole

path that is left for me to take. So by reading and practice I try to gain in quality of concentration and reflection this key to all progress. Now that's thrilling.

It's time to conclude this chapter about myself and to come back to those who have been reading this book in order to recover time. Because it invites you to begin *by devoting time to time*, you might wonder if this was not a trap.

Speaking of traps, I venture to say you have probably been in love. A little, a lot, in any case enough so that, suddenly, in a life that was already full, you found yourself making long telephone calls several times a day, dreaming of the image of the other person, walking together aimlessly through the streets, leaving work early. So where did you find the time to do all that? You cancelled what had suddenly become less important and gratifying.

The amorous shock reordered your priorities. You realized your time was less inflexible than you thought, that you in fact had some to spare.

The mastery of time may not bring you the pleasures of a grand passion, but it will bring the more subtle (and lasting) delights of personal progress.

Try considering it as the way to fall back in love with your life. Then, perhaps, the price of the hours you devote to it will seem comfortably within your means.

CONCLUSION:
THE ART OF TIME

❖

The Greeks were the first people to have a theory of art. They sought reasons and rules for those rare human creations that sustain our inner coherence. They concluded that five elements were necessary in art: order, equilibrium, contrast, unity, and harmony.

The importance of these elements has been minimally affected by the advent of technological civilization. Are they in fact anything other than the expression of our own profound yearnings and sources of satisfaction? They must apply to our style of life as well as the friezes of the Parthenon.

And if the expression "the art of time" is not an empty formula, it is because we may hope both to consider how these five qualities apply to time and to act so that this is very much our own work:

1. *Order,* because we need to know where our time is going. We have trouble in seizing it globally, and we organize and distribute it according to our capacity for analysis. Once the time structures chosen by us materialize and endure, confusion abates.

2. *Balance,* when we discover that letting our time be swallowed up in one principal activity (however gratifying) entails decay and ruptures in other areas. Scarce time is inevitably rationed among the main areas of interest in our lives, and it is we who decide how to distribute it. When this distribution is uneven, we will be the first to suffer the consequences.

3. *Contrast,* by accepting ourselves as we are, namely, not disposed to tolerate doing the same thing for long. To know how to alternate the mental and the physical, concentration and diversion, solitude and communication, action and retreat. This incessant movement constitutes the dance of life. Now, is not dance the oldest and most widespread of the arts?

4. *Unity,* for order is not compartmentalization, but the emergence of a view of the whole. Segmenting our life would be losing what life offers in the way of unexpected syntheses and fertile resonances. Modern time presents itself to us all cross-ruled. Only we, through concentration, can restore unity to it.

5. *Harmony,* in ancient Greek, meant "together." It is, of course, the joint product of the four preceding qualities. It is not definable, but felt. In the morning: "Does the day look promising?" In the evening: "Have

I used my time well?" Or at every instant, when we stick our head out the window of the present. Harmony is both the test of our mastery and its reward.

The art of time appears also as the first stage toward an art of living that implies, in addition to what has just been mentioned, the accomplishment of our plans. When we achieve even an average mastery of our time, our plans' chances of success take a giant leap.

At the start, the diciplines for reaching this will seem constraining. There is no need for fretting about this: it is merely a transitional stage, and it is so worth the trouble!

A little more time: isn't this the most beautiful and precious gift we can give ourselves?

Using the parallel with dieting one last time, the diet is initially experienced as hard: forgoing the foods we like (sugar, pasta, and so forth) and restricting our intake of the rest. Each meal is seen as a test of our willpower. Then one day, we are no longer tempted by the forbidden foods and we no longer want second helpings of the rest. We talk not about our diet, but about new eating habits.

Similarly here, the method's apparent goal is merely to help us use our days and weeks better. Its real goal is to help us internalize the form, flow, and value of our time.

When we have done this, we shall react to every element of life by sensing how it will fit into our time, weigh on it. At that point we will no longer need the method. It will have allowed us to reach a new level of awareness. We will be able to leave it by the roadside like a vehicle that has taken us to our destination.

It will be at our own pace that we make progress toward mastery. For this progress never stops, as long as we still have time to live.

FROM TIME TO TIME:
A Brief Anthology of Ideas

Henri Frédéric Amiel (Swiss writer, 1821–1881)
"Time is just the space between our memories. When we cease perceiving this space, time has vanished." *Diary*, January 21, 1866.

Louis Aragon (French poet and novelist, 1897–1982)
"Oh how the sky above will be clear and pure
In our absence and time
No clock will have
It will be beautiful." *Rooms*.

Jacques Attali (French presidential advisor, 1944–   )
"In the modern industrial age the key machine is not the steam engine, but the timepiece." *Stories of Time*.

"To be in power is to control the time of others and one's own." Ibid.

"To observe is to destroy and to go with the flow of time; to create is to construct and to stem the flow of time." Ibid.

Gaston Bachelard (French philosopher, 1884–1962)
"Time has but one reality, that of the instant. In other words, time is a reality confined to the instant and suspended between two voids." *The Intuition of the Instant.*

Honoré de Balzac (French novelist, 1799–1850)
"Time is the sole capital of people whose only fortune is their intelligence." *Lost Illusions.*

Charles Baudelaire (French poet, 1821–1867)
"One can forget time only by making use of it." *My Heart Laid Bare.*

Henri Bergson (French philosopher, 1859–1941)
"Time is invention or it is nothing at all." *Creative Evolution.*

Louis de Bonald (French political writer, 1754– 1840)
"There are people who do not know how to waste their time all by themselves. They are the scourge of active people."

Marie Bonaparte (French psychoanalyst, 1882–1962)
"Thus, time makes me and I make time."

Jorge Luis Borges (Argentine storywriter, 1899– 1987)
"Time is the substance I am made of. Time is a river that sweeps me along, but I am time; it is a tiger that rips me apart, but I am the tiger; it is a fire that consumes me, but I am the fire." *Other Inquisitions.*

Lewis Carroll, pseud. of Charles L. Dodgson (English mathematician and storywriter, 1832–1898)

"If you knew time as well as I do, " said the Hatter, "you wouldn't talk about wasting *it*. It's *him*." *Alice in Wonderland*.

Emile M. Cioran (Rumanian aphorist, 1911–   )

"My mission is to kill time and its in turn is to kill me. One is so comfortable among murderers." *Drawn and Quartered* (English translation by Richard Howard).

Paul Claudel (French writer and diplomat, 1868– 1955)

"It is not time that is lacking, it is we who are lacking it." *Partage de midi*.

Jean Cocteau (French dramatist, 1889–1963)

"The time of men is eternity folded." *The Infernal Machine*.

Denis Diderot (French encyclopedist, 1713–1784)

"Suppose an astronomer gave a geometrical proof that a thousand years from now the orbit of some planet will intersect the earth's orbit precisely at the point and moment where the earth was, and that this huge collision would destroy the earth; then lassitude will overcome all works; no ambition, no monuments, no poets, no historians, and perhaps not even any warmakers or wars. Each person would tend his garden and plant his cabbages. Without suspecting it, we are all marching to eternity." *Elements of Physiology*.

T. S. Eliot (American poet, 1888–1965)
"Because I know that time is always time
And place is always and only place
And what is actual is actual only for one time
And only for one place
I rejoice that things are as they are." *Ash Wednesday*.

Jean Giono (French writer, 1895–1970)
"We have forgotten that our only goal is to live and that we live each day and that at every hour of the day we are reaching our true goal if we are living. . . . The days are fruits and our role is to eat them." *Fullness of Days*.

E. Hall (1914–)
"The standardization of time is the basis of a classificatory system that rules life. Except for birth and death, all important activities are scheduled." *Beyond Culture*.

"In fact, being in a position to decide the use of one's time—and the hours one is present at the office—indicates that one has arrived." Ibid.

Friedrich Hegel (German philosopher, 1770–1831)
"Time, that pure anxiety/disquiet of life and that process of absolute distinction." *The Phenomenology of Spirit/Mind*.

Victor Hugo (French poet, novelist, and dramatist, 1802–1885)
"O time! Days of radiance! Dawn too early enraptured! Why does God thus put the best of life Right at the start?" *Interior Voices*.

Pierre Janet (French psychologist, 1859–1947)

"Will not man someday make progress in time similar to that he has made in space?" *From Anguish to Ecstasy*, Volume I.

Marcel Jouhandeau (French writer, 1888–1979)

"Because nothing is more precious than time, there is no greater generosity than to lose it without counting." *Journaliers* [*Everyday Occurrences*].

Jean de La Bruyère (French writer and moralist, 1645–1696)

"Persons who use their time ill are the first to complain of its brevity." "Judgements," *Characters*.

"Men's regrets about using poorly the time they have already lived do not always lead them to make better use of the time they have yet to live." *Ibid.* XI.

Marcus Aurelius Antoninus (Roman emperor and Stoic philosopher, 121–180 A.D.)

"Time is a sort of river of passing events, and strong is its current." *Meditations* IV.

Karl Marx (German political philosopher and socialist, 1818–1883)

"The capitalist steals the time that should be used for breathing free air and delighting in the sunlight." Quoted in "Histoires du Temps," Jacques Attali.

"Time is the field of human development." *Salary, Price, and Profit*.

Michel de Montaigne (French essayist, 1533–1592)

"It is possible that for persons who use their time well, knowledge and experience increase throughout life." *Essays*, Book I.

Charles de Montesquieu (French lawyer and political philosopher, 1689–1755)

"Lamentable, there is too short an interval between the time when one is too young and the time when one is too old." *My Thoughts*.

Paul Morand (French writer, 1888–1976)

One day, the hero of Paul Morand's novel *Man in a Hurry* meets Commodore Swift, the fastest man in the world and inventor of the Gunshot, a vehicle capable of hurtling over Salt Lake at a speed of eight hundred feet per second. But the commodore has been immobilized for more than four months waiting for the right combination of wind, humidity, the state of the ground— all the conditions required for the tricky operation to succeed. Speed must be a strange god for one to sacrifice everything to it, even time! The record holder for speed deserved to be famous under another name: the man who took fourteen and a half months to go one mile.

Napoleon (French emperor, 1769–1821)

"Time is the great art of man." *Letters to the King of Naples*, March 1, 1807.

Friedrich Nietzsche (German philosopher, 1844–1900)

"Time in itself is an absurdity: time exists only in relation to a sentient being." *The Philosopher's Book, Theoretical Studies.*

Blaise Pascal (French mathematician and philosopher, 1623–1662)

"Memory is necessary for all the operations of reason." *Thoughts.*

"We never keep to the present. We try to steal a march the future as if it were too slow in coming, or as if we could hasten its flow; or we recall the past to halt its retreat as if it were too rapid; so imprudent are we that we wander in times that are not ours, and give no thought to the only time that does belong to us." *Ibid.*

Charles Péguy (French writer, 1873–1914)

"Tell me how you treat the present, and I will tell you what kind of philosopher you are. ... If you connect the present, everything is connected. If you keep the present free, only then can the other freedoms be arranged or arranged well. If you sterilize the present, all is sterile, all is empty. If you keep the present fertile, only then can all the other fertilities be arranged, and arranged well."

Marcel Proust (French novelist, 1871–1922)

"Theoretically, we know that the earth turns, but in fact we do not notice this; the earth we tread seems not to move and we live in peace; in life, it is the same with time." "Within a Budding Grove," *The Remembrance of Things Past.*

Jean-Paul Sartre (French philosopher, dramatist, and novelist, 1905–1980)

"We don't want to miss anything in our time; perhaps there are finer times, but the present one is ours." *Situations* II.

Ettore Scola (1931–)

"Time is the most beautiful thing with its ruins, its thromboses, its vanished hopes, its illusions that die, and gives each breaking day a new illusion . . ."

Elsa Triolet (French writer, 1896–1970)

"We ought always to see ourselves as people who are going to die the next day. It is the time we think we have before us that kills." *Luna-Park*.

Voltaire (French writer, 1694–1778)

"Time is long enough to whoever takes advantage of it; He who works and thinks stretches its limits." *Discouse in Verse on Man.*

"The great Magus [or seer] proposed first this question: Of all the things in the world, which is the longest and shortest, the most quickest and the slowest, the most divisible and the most extensive, the most disregarded and the most regretted, without which nothing can happen, which devours everything that is little, and gives life everything that is great?

It was Itobad's turn to speak. He replied that a man like himself knew nothing of riddles and that it was enough for him to have conquered with great thrusts of his lance. Some said that the word for the riddle was fortune, others the earth, others light. Zadig said that it was time. Nothing is longer, he added, since it is the measure of eternity; nothing is shorter, since it is lacking in all our plans; nothing is slower for him who waits, nothing is quicker for him who enjoys; it extends to the infinitely little; all men disregard it, all men regret the loss of it; nothing happens without it; it makes forgotten everything unworthy of posterity, and it immortalizes the great things.

The assemble agreed that Zadig was right." *Zadig*.